Growing Marijuana

for Beginners

The Art and Science of
Growing Cannabis:
A Comprehensive Guide
for Novice Gardeners

Luca Morales

TABLE OF CONTENTS

INTRODUCTION

Why grow marijuana?

Individuals have been cultivating and using marijuana, also known as cannabis, for thousands of years. Growing marijuana has seen a rise in popularity recently, both for recreational and therapeutic uses. The option to grow marijuana requires serious thought, as well as an awareness of the potential advantages and driving forces behind this activity.

Marijuana has drawn a lot of interest because of its possible medical benefits. Numerous chemical compounds called cannabinoids, which have therapeutic properties, are present in the plant. Cannabidiol (CBD), one of the most well-known cannabinoids, has shown effectiveness in easing pain, decreasing inflammation, and helping to manage illnesses like epilepsy, multiple sclerosis, and chronic pain. Tetrahydrocannabinol (THC), another well-known cannabinoid that gives marijuana its psychoactive effects, has also showed effectiveness in treating PTSD, cancer, and glaucoma symptoms. People can directly access these medical advantages by growing their own marijuana, which can relieve their own or their loved ones' suffering.

Individuals have complete control over the cultivation process while growing marijuana at home, from seed selection through harvesting. This degree of control guarantees the product's quality. Numerous cannabis products sold commercially could come with pesticides, herbicides, or other potentially dangerous substances. By using organic production techniques to grow marijuana, people can completely eliminate the chance of coming into contact with dangerous toxins. Additionally, cultivation at home enables the personalization of growing parameters like light, temperature, and nutrients, producing a superior end product tailored to preferences.

Another significant reason why people decide to produce marijuana is the financial component. It can be expensive to buy marijuana from dispensaries or dealers, especially if you need it frequently for medical reasons. Individuals may significantly lower their costs by cultivating marijuana. Although equipment, seeds, and other supplies need an initial investment, the long-term savings are significant. Additionally, growing marijuana can be viewed as a pastime or an investment, with the possibility to generate revenue through the sale of extra crop.

Cannabis cultivation enables people to take charge of their own health. They become self-sufficient in supplying their cannabis requirements by growing their own plants. This freedom and empowerment are fostered by self-sufficiency, which lessens dependency on outside sources. Additionally, it enables people to experiment with various strains and types, customizing the growth process to meet their own needs, whether they be for therapeutic or recreational uses. Marijuana cultivation also fosters a greater awareness for the plant and its growth, connecting people closer to the natural world and the process of sustaining life.

Some people find that marijuana cultivation itself is therapeutic and joyful. It may be really gratifying to take care of plants, support their development, and watch them grow from seed to harvest. In general, gardening has been shown to lower stress, enhance mental health, and promote a connection with nature. As people see the results of their effort and get to experience using something they helped to grow, marijuana cultivation adds another dimension of fulfillment and happiness. For those looking for a hands-on and interesting activity, it can be a satisfying and fulfilling journey.

In conclusion, there are many reasons and advantages for choosing to produce marijuana. People find compelling reasons to start this path, from the therapeutic benefits it provides to the sense of self-sufficiency, financial savings, and delight obtained from caring for plants. Growing marijuana gives people a way to take control of their well-being and connect with nature, whether this is motivated by a need for quality control, practical considerations, or a desire for personal empowerment. The awareness of cannabis cultivation's potential advantages is expanding with interest in it, making it an appealing alternative for many.

Understanding the legal aspects

In many parts of the world, the legal environment surrounding marijuana cultivation is fast changing. As opinions against cannabis evolve, it is crucial for potential growers to have a thorough awareness of the legal aspects related to marijuana cultivation.

In various nations and regions, marijuana cultivation is not legal in all circumstances. While some regions have completely legalized the growth of marijuana for both medical and recreational purposes, others continue to enforce stringent restrictions. In certain locations, personal cultivation is allowed but is subject to restrictions on plant quantity or growing conditions. To maintain compliance and prevent legal implications, people must learn and understand the various laws and rules governing marijuana cultivation in their respective countries.

The legal system frequently makes a distinction between marijuana growing for medical and recreational purposes. Cannabis is grown for specialized therapeutic objectives in medicinal cultivation, as opposed to recreational cultivation, which is intended for personal consumption or other non-commercial uses. For medicinal production, several jurisdictions demand that people get licenses or permits, which frequently come with extra criteria like medical recommendations or verification. To ensure compliance with the intended use of marijuana growth, it is essential to comprehend the legal distinctions between recreational and therapeutic growing.

Getting the required licenses and permits is a crucial step in areas where marijuana growth is permitted. These permits control the cultivation process, provide quality control, and prevent unlicensed cultivation. Background checks, security measures, and adherence to particular cultivation standards may be needed in order to get licenses and permits. To legally engage in marijuana cultivation activities, one must get familiar with the application procedure and follow the appropriate regulations.

Zoning and location constraints are frequently involved in the legal issues of marijuana growth. Authorities at the federal, state, and local levels can designate certain locations or zones for marijuana growth. These rules are meant to protect the public, ensure safety, and preserve the integrity of the communities around while minimizing any potential negative effects. Cannabis growers must be aware of these zoning constraints and adhere to the designated locations or premises specified in the legal framework.

Numerous countries place restrictions on the number of plants or the total canopy area that may be grown for personal or professional use. These restrictions are in place to prevent illegal distribution, overproduction, and legal system abuse. To prevent legal penalties, it is crucial for cultivators to comprehend and carefully abide by these cultivation limits. The legality of the cultivation enterprise is put at risk if these regulations are broken because doing so can result in fines, penalties, or even criminal prosecution.

The legal framework frequently places an emphasis on rules for marijuana cultivation safety and quality control. These rules are designed to guarantee that what is grown is safe for consumption and free of pollutants like pesticides or heavy metals. To preserve consumer safety and uphold the integrity of the legal marijuana market, compliance with quality control standards, including testing and labeling laws, is essential. Growers must be aware of the precise quality control laws that pertain to them and take the required steps to adhere to the established standards.

It is crucial to understand that marijuana laws and policies are dynamic and always evolving. Based on scientific study, public opinion, and societal demands, governments and regulatory organizations continuously analyze and revise the legal framework surrounding marijuana cultivation. In order to adapt and continue to comply with the law, growers must keep up with these legislative changes and comprehend the potential effects on their operations.

In conclusion, those looking to engage in marijuana cultivation must have a solid understanding of its legal implications. In-depth investigation and compliance are required due to the complexity of international legal variances, licensing and permit requirements, zoning and location constraints, cultivation limits, quality control and safety requirements, and the dynamic nature of legislation and policy changes. Cultivators may assure legal compliance, safeguard their interests, and contribute to the responsible and sustainable growth of the marijuana sector by understanding the legal framework.

Setting realistic expectations

Getting started with marijuana cultivation can be a thrilling endeavor. Whether motivated by a need for personal use, potential medical advantages, or a developing interest in horticulture, it is essential to start out with reasonable expectations. Understanding the difficulties, demands on your time, and other factors involved in marijuana cultivation will not only help you avoid disappointment, but will also lay the groundwork for a fruitful and satisfying experience.

Cannabis growing is a complex process that calls for knowledge, expertise, and experience. It is important to understand that raising high-quality marijuana plants requires practice, effort, and time. On their journey, novice cultivators may face obstacles and setbacks including pest infestations, nutrient deficiencies, or environmental changes. Cannabis growers will be better able to overcome challenges with patience and perseverance if they have realistic expectations about the learning curve involved in the industry and are aware that it takes time to become an expert and perfect cultivating methods.

Growing marijuana requires a significant effort and time commitment. The process might take months from germination to harvest. To keep an eye on plant health, modify the environment, and handle any potential problems, daily care and attention are required.

Schedules for cultivators must include enough time for recurring operations like watering, trimming, and keeping track of plant development. Setting realistic expectations about the time and work needed to properly grow marijuana is essential for maintaining a commitment throughout the whole growing cycle.

Cannabis cultivation yields can vary depending on a number of variables, including genetics, growth techniques, environmental factors, and grower skill. It's crucial to have reasonable expectations about the prospective yield when taking all the relevant factors into account. While sizable harvests are feasible, it's equally important to understand that yield changes can happen as a result of unforeseen conditions. The end result may be impacted by variables like plant health, nutrient deficits, and pest infestations. Cultivators can concentrate on improving their cultivation techniques while appreciating the process itself by knowing and accepting the unpredictability in yield.

Several environmental elements, including temperature, humidity, light, and air flow, have an impact on marijuana cultivation. These elements have a big effect on how a plant grows and develops. Realistic expectations must be made with regard to the constraints imposed by the immediate environment. Growers should evaluate their growing spaces and comprehend how they could impact the cultivation process. Additional lighting or climate control methods can be required in areas with harsh climates or little access to natural sunlight. Cultivators can improve their growing conditions and increase their chances of success by being aware of and working within environmental constraints.

Understanding the legal framework pertaining to marijuana cultivation is also necessary for setting realistic expectations. Cannabis growers need to be aware of local laws and rules governing marijuana cultivation, such as limitations on the number of plants that may be grown, possession limits, and licensing procedures. Failure to follow the law may result in legal consequences and setbacks for cultivation efforts. Cultivators can ensure a legal and compliant cultivation process by becoming familiar with the relevant rules and regulations.

Costs associated with marijuana cultivation include equipment, supplies, seeds or clones, as well as continuous costs like energy and water. Setting reasonable expectations for the necessary financial investment is crucial. There are up-front costs associated with setting up a proper grow space and obtaining the appropriate equipment, even though growing marijuana can result in cost savings compared to purchasing from dispensaries. Additionally, the budget needs to account for continuing costs like utilities and maintenance. Cultivators can plan efficiently and prevent financial difficulties by creating a realistic budget and being aware of the accompanying expenditures.

Every grower has different tastes and objectives when it comes to growing marijuana. Setting realistic expectations in line with personal objectives is essential, whether the goal is to create high-quality medicinal strains, test various genetic variations, or simply enjoy the gardening process. A fulfilling and enjoyable cultivation experience will be guaranteed by understanding and embracing individual motivations and limitations.

In conclusion, it's crucial for anyone considering starting a marijuana cultivation to have realistic expectations. Cultivators can approach the process with a balanced viewpoint by considering the learning curve, time commitment, environmental restrictions, legal issues, unpredictability in yield, cultivation costs, and personal preferences and aspirations. A successful and gratifying cultivation experience is built on realistic expectations, which also encourage patience, determination, and a deeper understanding of the complexities of marijuana growth.

CHAPTER
I
Cannabis Basics

What is cannabis?

Cannabis, usually referred to as marijuana, is a complex and fascinating plant that has captivated people's interest for ages. Cannabis has a unique place in society because of its long history of use for therapeutic and recreational purposes as well as its present place in scientific research and alternative therapies.

The Cannabaceae family includes the flowering plant known as cannabis. Cannabis ruderalis, a less frequent third species, is one of the two main species of cannabis, along with Cannabis sativa and Cannabis indica. These species are further divided into different strains, each of which displays unique traits, growth patterns, and chemical compositions.

The cannabis plant has a number of distinctive characteristics that add to its special traits. The plant is made up of many different components, such as roots, stems, leaves, flowers (buds), and seeds. Usually compound, the leaves have leaflets with palmate or digitate leaf edges and serrated edges. The majority of the plant's medicinal and recreational benefits come from the flowers, which have the highest cannabinoid concentrations.

The chemical composition of cannabis, notably the presence of cannabinoids, is one of its distinguishing characteristics. Cannabinoids are a class of chemical compounds that interact with the endocannabinoid system of the human body to affect a number of physiological functions. Tetrahydrocannabinol (THC) and cannabidiol (CBD) are the two most widely used cannabinoids. THC is the component responsible for the psychoactive effects that are typically associated with marijuana, whereas CBD has gained attention due to the potential therapeutic properties it possesses.

Different cannabis strains have distinctive impacts on the body and mind because they have different cannabinoid compositions. The psychoactive effects of THC-dominant strains, which cause euphoria, relaxation, and altered sensory perception, are well recognized. Conversely, strains that are CBD-dominant are frequently linked to non-intoxicating effects like relaxation, pain reduction, and possibly anti-inflammatory advantages. The combination of various cannabinoids and their ratios inside a specific strain leads to the wide spectrum of effects that cannabis users encounter.

Cannabis has been used medicinally for a very long time, going back thousands of years. The endocannabinoid system, which controls a number of biological functions, including mood, pain perception, and immune response, is where the plant's therapeutic potential rests. According to research, cannabis may be useful in treating a variety of diseases, including multiple sclerosis, epilepsy, chronic pain, and nausea brought on by chemotherapy. To fully comprehend the therapeutic uses of cannabis and its components, further research is still required.

Cannabis has long been used recreationally as a way to unwind, socialize, and experience altered states of consciousness. Euphoria, enhanced sensory experiences, and relaxation can all be brought on by THC's psychoactive effects. Recreational cannabis use ranges widely, from social use on occasion to regular use for stress relief or creative endeavors.

Cannabis has a variety of industrial uses outside of its medical and recreational purposes. Hemp, a versatile material used in textiles, paper, construction materials, and biofuels, can be made from the plant's fibers. Products made from hemp, such as CBD oil and hemp seed oil, are becoming more and more well-liked because of their possible health advantages and nutritional worth.

Cannabis is legal in a wide range of places around the world and in different countries. While some nations have legalized cannabis for both medical and recreational use, others have stringent restrictions or outright bans. As the possible advantages and disadvantages of cannabis usage have been more investigated and comprehended, the shifting attitudes about cannabis have prompted ongoing discussions and reforms in many locations.

In conclusion, cannabis is a remarkable plant that has fascinated people throughout history because of its intricate botanical structure, complicated chemical composition, and wide range of applications. Cannabis continues to capture the curiosity of researchers, enthusiasts, and governments around the world because of its potential medical benefits as well as its recreational use and industrial possibilities. For creating informed discussions, encouraging responsible usage, and realizing the full potential of the plant for societal good, it is crucial to comprehend the botanical composition of cannabis and the variety of impacts it can have.

Different types of cannabis strains

The cannabis plant has a wide range of strains, each with their own distinct characteristics, flavors, and effects. Cannabis enthusiasts have a wide range of options to consider, from stimulating and uplifting sativas to calming and sedating indicas, and the hybrid strains that combine the best of both worlds.

Sativa strains are well-liked options for daytime consumption because of their uplifting and invigorating qualities. These strains, which are equatorial in origin, often produce tall, slender plants with narrow leaves. Sativas are frequently thought to have uplifting and cerebral effects that foster creativity, concentration, and sociability. The sativa varieties Durban Poison, Jack Herer, and Sour Diesel are among well-known examples. People looking for a euphoric and invigorating high as well as those hoping to find some relief from sadness, exhaustion, and mood disorders favor sativa strains.

Indica strains are preferred for use at night because of their calming and sedating properties, which encourage rest and sleep. Indica plants typically have shorter, bushier growth and broader leaves because they are native to harsh climates. Indicas are frequently thought to have body-focused effects that relax the muscles, relieve pain, and promote tranquillity. Indica strains that are well-known include Afghan Kush, Granddaddy Purple, and Northern Lights. People looking for sleep help, pain treatment, and stress alleviation prefer indica strains.

Sativa and indica plants are crossed to create hybrid strains, which combine the greatest traits of both plant species. Breeders can produce breeds with certain traits and consequences through hybridization, satisfying a variety of preferences. Depending on the genetic background, hybrid strains can be either indica- or sativa-dominant or balanced (50/50). With some hybrid strains favoring cerebral stimulation and others favoring physical relaxation, they offer a wide range of benefits. Popular hybrid strains include Girl Scout Cookies, OG Kush, and Blue Dream. Hybrid strains offer flexibility, enabling people to select a combination of effects that best meets their needs.

Cannabis strains known as landraces are those that have developed spontaneously, unaided by human interference, over many years in a particular geographic area. These strains are local to their particular areas and distinguished by their distinctive genetic profile, flavors, and effects. The landrace strains Acapulco Gold, Malawi Gold, and Hindu Kush are a few examples. For their authenticity and preservation of historical cannabis genetics, landrace strains are highly valuable. They frequently have distinctive terpene profiles and effects that are a reflection of the original environment.

Non-intoxicating cannabinoid CBD (cannabidiol) is well-known for its possible therapeutic advantages. High-CBD strains are developed to have higher ratios of CBD to THC. While limiting the psychoactive effects of THC, these strains offer possible medicinal effects like pain alleviation, anxiety reduction, and anti-inflammatory qualities. Charlotte's Web, Harlequin, and AC/DC are a few varieties that have a high CBD content. People looking for cannabis' possible medical benefits without its euphoric effects prefer high-CBD strains.

Tetrahydrocannabinol, or THC, is the main psychoactive cannabinoid in cannabis and is what gives the plant its characteristically euphoric and intoxicating effects. High-THC strains are grown to have higher THC concentrations, resulting in strong and mind-altering effects. These strains have potent cerebral effects as well as euphoria, relaxation, and enhanced sensory perception. Gorilla Glue #4, Bruce Banner, and Ghost OG are a few examples of strains with a high THC content. Recreational consumers prefer high-THC strains because they get a stronger, more psychedelic high from them.

Unique and rare cultivars that have distinctive qualities, flavors, or effects are referred to as specialty strains. These strains are frequently the result of meticulous breeding, selection, and genetic modification to provide novel experiences or satisfy certain tastes. Exotic tastes, unusual terpene profiles, or extraordinary potency are some characteristics of specialty strains. Cookies and Cream, Purple Haze, and Pineapple Express are a few specialty strains. Cannabis enthusiasts have the chance to push the limits of the cannabis experience by experimenting with novel flavors and effects due to specialty strains.

Crossbreeding with the cannabis ruderalis, a subspecies of cannabis known for its capacity to automatically flower depending on age rather than light cycles, produces autoflowering strains. These strains are preferred since they are simple to grow and don't require tight light schedules to start flowering. Compared to regular photoperiod strains, autoflowering strains are often smaller and have a shorter lifetime. For those looking for quicker harvests or novice growers, they offer an affordable option. Lowryder, Northern Light Automatic, and Amnesia Haze Automatic are a few autoflowering strains.

In conclusion, there are many unique and diverse cannabis strains available, giving cannabis enthusiasts a wide range of options. Each type of cannabis strain offers a unique combination of properties, aromas, and effects, from the energizing sativas to the calming indicas, the adaptable hybrids to the rare landrace and speciality strains. Individuals can personalize their cannabis experience to their preferences and intended outcomes by having a thorough understanding of the various cannabis strains. There is a cannabis strain waiting to be discovered and appreciated, whether you're looking for pain relief, creativity, relaxation, or a distinctive flavor profile.

Understanding THC and CBD

Cannabinoids, which are found in large quantities in the cannabis plant, interact with the endocannabinoid system of the human body. Tetrahydrocannabinol (THC) and cannabidiol (CBD) are two of these cannabinoids that have drawn the most interest because of their distinct characteristics and potential medical uses.

Chemical Structures:

a. THC: Tetrahydrocannabinol, also known as THC, is the primary psychoactive cannabinoid found in cannabis. It is what causes the euphoric and intoxicated effects that are frequently linked to marijuana use. 21 carbon atoms, 30 hydrogen atoms, and 2 oxygen atoms make up the chemical structure of THC. Its molecular formula is C21H30O2.

b. CBD: A non-intoxicating cannabinoid, cannabidiol is becoming known for its potential therapeutic uses. Compared to THC, CBD has a somewhat different chemical composition. Similar to THC, it has 21 carbon atoms, 30 hydrogen atoms, and 2 oxygen atoms. These atoms are arranged differently, though, and this causes different effects on the body.

Effects on the Body and Mind:

a. THC: When THC enters the body, it binds to cannabinoid receptors in the endocannabinoid system, especially CB1 receptors. Numerous physiological and psychoactive effects are produced by this combination. Dopamine is a neurotransmitter linked to pleasure and reward. THC promotes dopamine production, which results in sensations of euphoria and relaxation. Memory, coordination, and perception are also impacted. Depending on the user, dose, strain, and mode of intake, THC's psychoactive effects may differ.

b. CBD: In contrast to THC, CBD does not connect to cannabinoid receptors as strongly. Instead, it indirectly affects the endocannabinoid system by interacting with other non-cannabinoid receptors and regulating receptor activity. It is thought that CBD has a more modest mental impact and is frequently referred to as non-intoxicating or non-psychoactive. It could provide calming effects, ease stress and anxiety, and possibly have analgesic and anti-inflammatory properties. The potential anticonvulsant, neuroprotective, and anti-nausea effects of CBD have also been studied.

Medical Applications:

a. THC: Because of its intoxicating effects, THC has been used for a variety of medical conditions. It is frequently recommended to treat illnesses like chronic pain, chemotherapy-induced nausea and vomiting, multiple sclerosis muscular spasms, and appetite stimulation in HIV/AIDS patients. THC has also demonstrated promise in treating glaucoma, lowering intraocular pressure, and enhancing sleep.

b. CBD: CBD has drawn a lot of attention due to its potential medicinal uses for treating a range of medical ailments. It is frequently used as an additional epilepsy medication, especially when seizures are resistant to other forms of therapy. It has been shown that CBD has antipsychotic characteristics and may help with anxiety, sadness, and post-traumatic stress disorder (PTSD) symptoms. It has also been researched for its possible anti-inflammatory qualities, which may help treat diseases like inflammatory bowel disease and arthritis.

Differences between THC and CBD:

a. THC, the main psychoactive compound in cannabis, is what gives users a "high" or intoxication feeling. Contrarily, CBD does not get users high and does not have the same psychoactive effects as THC.

b. Legal Status: THC is categorized as a controlled substance and is subject to legal limitations in several nations. On the other hand, hemp, a type of cannabis with a low THC content, is frequently used to make CBD, which is frequently legal in many jurisdictions.

c. THC's short-term negative effects include accelerated heartbeat, dry mouth, red eyes, and memory and coordination problems. On the other hand, studies have found that CBD is generally well tolerated and causes few negative effects.

d. Drug Testing: Because THC is frequently detected in routine drug testing, using it can lead to a positive drug test. If CBD is made from hemp, it is unlikely to cause a positive drug test result.

The entourage effect describes how THC and CBD interact with other cannabis compounds like terpenes and other cannabinoids. According to the entourage effect, a cannabis plant's many components work better together to create medicinal effects than the plant's individual cannabinoids. This interaction between the two substances may be the reason why some people prefer products that include both THC and CBD or choose whole-plant extracts over separate chemicals.

The two main cannabis cannabinoids, THC and CBD, each have distinctive characteristics and potential medical uses. While CBD is recognized for being non-intoxicating and having potential therapeutic uses across a range of medical ailments, THC is known for its euphoric effects and has been used for medicinal purposes. People can make educated judgments about cannabis usage and explore the possible advantages of these fascinating compounds by knowing how THC and CBD differ from one another and how their effects differ on the body, mind, and environment.

Cannabis plant anatomy

The cannabis plant is a marvel of nature because of its lengthy history and wide range of uses. Understanding the structure of the cannabis plant is crucial for appreciating its complexity and potential. The anatomy of the cannabis plant, from the roots that support it to the ground to the complex forms of its leaves, flowers, and trichomes, holds the key to releasing its enormous therapeutic and recreational potential.

The roots of the cannabis plant serve important purposes at the beginning of their existence. The plant's roots anchor it in the ground and offer support and stability. They enable the plant to grow and thrive by absorbing water and nutrients from the soil. To enhance nutrient uptake, cannabis roots can reach far below the surface of the soil. Additionally, roots engage in symbiotic interactions with beneficial fungi to create mycorrhizal associations, which improve nutrient uptake and offer disease defense.

The cannabis plant's stem connects the roots to the leaves and flowers and serves as a structural support. Transport of water, nutrients, and carbohydrates is made possible as well as stability inside the plant. The vascular system, which consists of xylem and phloem tissues, is likewise housed in the stem. Phloem carries sugars made during photosynthesis to areas of growth and storage, while xylem carries water and nutrients from the roots to the rest of the plant.

Cannabis leaves are recognizable and iconic. Because they are compound leaves, their many leaflets are joined by a central stalk called a petiole. Depending on the cannabis strain, the number and shape of the leaflets can change. Cannabis leaves are essential to the process of photosynthesis, which is how plants turn light energy into chemical energy. They house the stomata, tiny holes on the surface of the leaf that promote gas exchange, including the reception of carbon dioxide and release of oxygen, and contain chlorophyll, the pigment that absorbs sunlight.

The points on a stem known as nodes are where leaves or branches first appear. They are essential in determining the cannabis plant's general structure and growth pattern. On the other hand, internodes are the areas between nodes. Cannabis strains can differ in the length of their internodes, which can change the height and branching pattern of the plant. In order to maximize plant training methods like pruning and topping, cultivators can benefit from understanding the arrangement of nodes and internodes.

The most cherished and sought-after portion of the cannabis plant is its flowers, which are also referred to as buds. They have the highest levels of terpenes, a class of aromatic compounds, as well as cannabinoids like THC and CBD. The cannabis plant's reproductive structures are its flowers, which include both the male and female reproductive organs. Cannabinoids and terpenes are produced by the resinous trichomes that are produced by female flowers. Cannabis flowers can differ significantly among strains in terms of size, density, and resin output.

Cannabis flowers, leaves, and stems have microscopic, hair-like structures called trichomes covering their surfaces. They are the epicenters of terpene and cannabinoid production. Trichomes perform a number of tasks, including as defending the plant from pests, lowering water loss, and perhaps discouraging herbivores. The largest levels of terpenes and cannabinoids are found in the glandular trichomes, also known as resin glands. Different cannabis strains' distinctive flavors, aromas, and therapeutic properties are influenced by these sticky structures.

The cannabis plant produces a wide variety of chemical compounds, such as terpenes and cannabinoids. The trichomes in the resin glands of the flowers are where cannabinoids, like THC and CBD, are formed. Terpenes, on the other hand, are fragrant substances that give cannabis its unique smells and odors. Additionally formed in the trichomes, they contribute to the entourage effect and raise the plant's overall medicinal potential. Different cannabis strains have various effects and properties that are due to the interaction of terpenes and cannabinoids.

There are two distinct leaf kinds found on cannabis plants, each with a unique place and use. The larger, more prominent leaves that develop on the plant's stems and branches are known as fan leaves. They shade the lowest portions of the plant and are in charge of photosynthesis. As opposed to this, sugar leaves are smaller and develop closer to the flowers. Trichomes are also present in these leaves, which help the plant produce resin. Because sugar leaves have a lesser THC concentration than marijuana flowers, they are frequently cut before being consumed or extracted.

Cannabis plant environment and production methods have an impact on its anatomy. Cannabis can grow in a variety of environments and climates. Cannabis plants may grow shorter and stockier in colder climates to endure harsh conditions. In order to maximize airflow and lessen heat stress, plants may have longer internodes in regions with higher temperatures. Understanding these environmental adaptations can help growers improve their methods of cultivation and choose the best cannabis strains for the conditions at hand.

The versatility, complexity, and beauty of the cannabis plant are demonstrated by its anatomical structure. Each part of the plant, from the roots that hold it to the ground to the delicate trichomes that create cannabinoids and terpenes, is essential to its development, growth, and therapeutic potential. Understanding the cannabis plant's anatomy helps growers, researchers, and enthusiasts make the most of the plant's potential for industrial, recreational, and medical uses while also increasing their understanding of this amazing botanical marvel.

CHAPTER
II
Getting Started

Choosing the right location

Selecting an ideal location for the cultivation of cannabis is important and can have a big impact on how successful your endeavor is. The site you choose—whether it's an indoor setup or an outdoor garden—plays a critical part in creating the perfect conditions for healthy plant growth and maximum output.

The climate and environmental factors are among the most crucial factors to take into account when choosing a location for cannabis growth. During the growing season, cannabis plants need warm temperatures, whereas during the flowering stage, they need cooler temperatures. In your selected area, take into account variables like the typical temperature, humidity levels, rainfall patterns, and wind exposure. In order to ensure optimal growth and avoid potential problems like mold or heat stress, it is important to understand the particular environment requirements of the cannabis strains you have chosen.

Sunlight exposure is essential for cultivation of cannabis outdoors. For healthy growth and the best resin production, cannabis plants need a minimum of 6 to 8 hours of direct sunlight each day. Consider issues like tree cover, nearby structures, and shadowing that may block sunlight when choosing an outdoor cultivation area. The majority of the day's sunlight falls on south-facing locations, whereas north-facing locations may see greater shade. In order to make sure your plants receive enough light for photosynthesis, you should also consider the angle and strength of the sun at various times of the day.

When selecting a location for cannabis growing, security and privacy are essential factors to take into account. Outdoor cannabis gardens may draw unwelcome attention or risk theft, depending on the laws in your location. Considerations should be made for things like visibility from the road, proximity to nearby houses, and the potential for security measures. Indoor cultivation gives you more control over security and privacy, but you might still need to take additional precautions like access controls and surveillance systems.

Cannabis growing requires good drainage and easy access to water. Make sure the place you've chosen has a dependable water source that can be reached quickly for irrigation needs. Take into account the availability of water rights, the quality of the water, and any regulatory limitations on water use. In order to avoid root rot and prevent waterlogging, good drainage is also essential. Raised beds or the installation of drainage systems may be required if the land has poor natural drainage in order to protect the health of your cannabis plants.

Plant health and productivity are greatly influenced by the kind and composition of the soil at your cultivation location. To determine the pH level, nutrient content, and soil structure, conduct soil testing. Cannabis plants prefer soil that drains well and has a pH between 6 and 7.5. Compost, perlite, or coco coir are examples of amendments that can be added to poor soil to increase drainage and nutrient retention. As an alternative, raised beds or container gardening can be used to regulate the soil conditions.

Researching and comprehending local laws and zoning restrictions is crucial before choosing a location for cannabis cultivation. Cannabis production is governed by a variety of laws in different jurisdictions, including limitations on plant quantity, setback regulations, security precautions, and licensing or permission procedures. To avoid legal problems and obstacles in your cultivation efforts, make sure that your chosen location complies with all relevant laws and regulations.

Take into account the location's accessibility, especially if you intend to transfer tools, supplies, or cannabis-infused goods. Road accessibility, closeness to transportation hubs, and the accessibility of utilities like electricity and water are all significant considerations. Consider the infrastructure needs for your cultivation setup as well, including whether it is an indoor facility that needs ventilation, lighting, and climate control systems or an outdoor garden that needs fencing, irrigation, and storage facilities.

Examine the area around the spot you've chosen, taking into account any potential contaminant or interference sources. Avoid regions where there is a lot of pollution, industrial activity, or chemical runoff because these things can affect how well your cannabis crop grows. Likewise, keep an eye out for nearby agricultural businesses that might be using pesticides or herbicides that could drift onto your plants. Maintaining the integrity of your cultivation site involves evaluating the air quality, proximity to hazardous pollutants, and potential sources of cross-pollination (if cultivating feminized seeds).

In conclusion, picking the ideal place for cannabis production is an essential decision that lays the groundwork for effective and fruitful cultivation activities. You can establish the ideal setting for healthy plant growth and maximum harvests by taking into account aspects like climate, sunlight exposure, security, water access, soil quality, local rules, accessibility, and the surrounding environment. You may position yourself for a satisfying and successful cannabis farming adventure by making thoughtful decisions and taking these important factors into account.

Indoor vs. outdoor cultivation

The production of cannabis presents the grower with a diverse range of opportunities, the two most common of which are indoor and outdoor growing. Growers need to carefully analyze the advantages and drawbacks of each technique because each one has its own unique set of benefits and considerations.

Growing cannabis indoor in a controlled setting, such as a grow room or a greenhouse, is referred to as indoor cultivation. This approach provides a number of benefits and things to think about, including the following:

One of the most major advantages of growing cannabis indoors is the increased degree of environmental control that is available. Growers have the ability to fine-tune environmental conditions such as temperature, humidity, light intensity, and photoperiod in order to produce the ideal conditions for plant development. Because of this management, it is feasible to cultivate throughout the entire year independent of the external weather conditions. This makes it possible to keep consistent quality and yields.

When opposed to growing plants outdoors, indoor horticulture offers gardeners increased levels of both protection and privacy. The atmosphere is monitored and controlled, so there is less of a chance of theft or unwanted attention, as well as potential problems with the law. Growers are able to secure their investments and keep their peace of mind if access is restricted, security measures are put into place, and growing activities are conducted in a discreet manner.

Growing plants indoors reduces the likelihood of damage from insects and illnesses that are more common in outdoor cultivation. Growers have the ability to avoid the entry of new diseases and pests into their crops by practicing strict control over the growing environment and adhering to rigorous cleanliness standards. This makes the growing process easier to control and more predictable, which in turn reduces the amount of pesticides that are required and improves the plants' overall health.

Growers have the opportunity to maximize the potential yield of their plants through the use of a variety of techniques, such as high-intensity lighting, hydroponic or aeroponic systems, and training methods such as topping or SCROG (Screen of Green). These techniques are utilized in indoor cultivation. Growers have the ability to attain numerous harvests in a single year and perhaps larger yields as compared to those achieved by outdoor growth if they create the ideal growing conditions and make use of modern cultivation techniques.

The greater initial and ongoing expenditures that are connected with constructing and maintaining a controlled environment are one of the main considerations that go into the decision to cultivate plants indoor. It is possible for the cost of equipment, including grow lights, ventilation systems, climate control systems, and electricity consumption, to be significant. In addition, ongoing costs like rent, utilities, and maintenance are factors that go into determining the total cost of operations.

Outdoor cultiavtion, also known as natural cultivation, is the process of cultivating cannabis in natural settings outdoors, making use of the sun and the weather as they occur naturally. This approach also has its own individual set of benefits and factors to consider, including the following:

When plants are grown outdoors, they are able to harness the power of the sun, which provides natural light that is abundant in a wide spectrum of wavelengths necessary for healthy plant growth. When plants are exposed to natural sunlight, they are able to strengthen their structures, which may result in enhanced cannabinoid production and larger yields. Natural sunlight is both free and abundant.

When compared to cultivation done indoors, growing plants outdoor may result in lower overall costs. Growers can cut down on or eliminate some of the costs associated with energy, lighting, and environmental control systems by making use of natural resources such as sunlight and rainwater. This may be of particular benefit to growers working on a small scale or who have restricted access to financial resources.

It is generally agreed that cultivating plants outdoor is preferable from an ecological and sustainable perspective. As a result of its reduced reliance on artificial lighting and climate control systems, it lowers the amount of carbon emissions that are connected with indoor production. In addition, the natural soil and microbial variety seen in outdoor conditions can lead to plants that are in better health and have a profile of terpenes that is closer to their natural state.

Growing plants outdoor exposes them to a variety of environmental variables over which producers have little control. Alterations in the weather, shifts in temperature, the presence of pests and illnesses are all threats to the plants. In addition, because the growing season is constrained by the natural cycles of sunlight, there is often just one harvest per year, although this number might vary greatly from region to region. Growers have additional responsibilities, including ensuring that they comply with any municipal legislation and zoning restrictions that may be relevant to outdoor growing.

Outdoor production enables access to a wider variety of cannabis genotypes and strains than their indoor counterparts. Outdoor cultivation can increase the expression of distinctive qualities, terpene profiles, and flavors that may be unique to a particular location or climate. This is accomplished by exposing plants to the natural climatic conditions and seasonal changes that occur in their native environment.

In conclusion, the decision between cultivating cannabis indoors or outdoors is determined by a number of criteria, such as the amount of accessible space, the available budget, the desired yield, the climate conditions, and any personal preferences that may come into play. Indoor cultivation provides greater control, safety, and the possibility of greater yields, but it also comes with higher expenditures for both starting and ongoing operations. Outdoor cultivation is advantageous in that it makes use of natural resources, ensures sustainability, and may result in lower costs; nevertheless, it is also subject to external conditions and has a finite growing season. Ultimately, growers are responsible for conducting an in-depth analysis of their objectives, available resources, and the environmental factors in their growing environment in order to select the production method that will best meet their requirements. Cannabis farmers are able to make educated judgments and embark on fruitful journeys toward profitable cannabis growing when they have a thorough awareness of the benefits and drawbacks associated with both indoor and outdoor cultivation.

Required equipment and tools

The growth of cannabis successfully demands the utilization of suitable equipment and tools in order to produce ideal growing conditions, maintain good plant health, and maximize harvests. The proper cultivation tools are absolutely necessary, and their importance ranges from the most fundamental need to the most advanced innovations.

It is essential to cultivate an ideal growing environment in order to foster robust plant growth and get maximum harvests. The following pieces of equipment are required in order to preserve the optimal conditions at all times:

When cultivating plants indoors or as supplemental lighting in greenhouses, grow lights are an absolute necessity. Intense light output is provided by high-intensity discharge (HID) lights such as metal halide (MH) and high-pressure sodium (HPS) bulbs. These lights are appropriate for use throughout the flowering and vegetative stages of plant growth. Light-emitting diodes, sometimes known as LEDs, have become increasingly popular as a result of their low energy consumption and adaptable spectrum output.

It is absolutely necessary to have adequate air circulation and ventilation in order to keep a healthy growing environment. Temperature, humidity, and air quality can all be more easily managed with the use of ventilation systems that include exhaust fans, intake fans, and carbon filters. They allow for the circulation of fresh air, remove excess heat and moisture, and prevent the development of stale air, which can lead to problems like as the growth of mold or the infestation of insects.

In order to keep the environment in a consistent state, climate control systems, which may include temperature and humidity controls, are essential. Growers are given the ability to control and monitor the levels of temperature and humidity within their facilities, ensuring that plants are able to flourish within the ideal range. Thermostats, air conditioners, dehumidifiers, and humidifiers are all possible components of these systems.

It is crucial for good plant growth to have irrigation that is both consistent and accurate. The distribution of water and nutrients to the root systems of plants can be facilitated in an effective and regulated manner through the use of irrigation systems like drip irrigation and automated watering systems. They contribute to the prevention of overwatering as well as water waste and guarantee that water is distributed evenly throughout the growing medium.

When it comes to the everyday cultivation duties that are necessary to ensure adequate plant care and maintenance, numerous tools are required. The following equipment is required for successfully cultivating cannabis:

Trimming leaves and branches, as well as preserving the overall structure of the plant, requires the use of pruning shears and scissors. They contribute to the reduction of superfluous foliage, the improvement of air circulation, and the redistribution of energy towards the growth of buds.

In order to monitor and modify the pH and nutrient levels in the growing medium, pH and EC (electrical conductivity) meters are absolutely necessary pieces of equipment. The ideal pH range, which normally falls somewhere between 5.5 and 6.5, should be maintained in order to promote optimal nutrient uptake and to prevent nutritional deficiencies or toxicities.

The pH of the water or nutrient solution can be adjusted to the desired range using solutions that either increase or decrease the pH. In order to increase the pH, pH up solution is added, and pH down solution is used in order to decrease it.

Trellis netting and plant supports offer cannabis plants with the necessary structural support, particularly when the plants are in the flowering stage. They assist in the training of the plants, prevent the branches from bending or breaking under the weight of the flowers, and ensure an even distribution of light for improved bud growth.

The trimming procedure can be made more effective with the use of trimming trays that come equipped with built-in screens or sifters. These trays catch trichomes and help keep the workspace clean. Drying racks provide a designated space for drying harvested buds.

They provide air circulation, which is necessary for proper drying and helps reduce the risk of mold and mildew growth.

Consistent analysis and monitoring of the most important factors are necessary for ensuring the health and productivity of cannabis plants. The following pieces of equipment are helpful in carrying out this process:

The pH level of the nutrient solution, soil, or water supply can be determined with the help of a pH testing kit, which typically comprises of test strips or liquid solutions. Testing the pH of the water on a regular basis helps to maintain healthy levels of nutrient absorption and helps prevent nutritional imbalances.

The nutrient concentration in the water or nutrient solution can be measured with a total dissolved solids (TDS) or electrical conductivity (EC) meter. It helps ensure precise dosing of nutrients and prevents either overfeeding or underfeeding from occurring.

The temperature of the growth environment can be measured with a thermometer, while the humidity levels can be determined with a hygrometer. Monitoring these parameters helps to maintain the appropriate range for plant growth, which in turn helps to prevent problems such as heat stress and the formation of mold.

Growers can better manage their lighting systems and make certain that their plants receive enough light levels for optimal development and photosynthesis with the assistance of a light meter, which detects the intensity of the light in the growing area.

In conclusion, the production of cannabis necessitates the utilization of a diverse selection of important pieces of equipment and tools in order to provide the best possible growing conditions and obtain the highest possible yields. In the process of cultivating plants, each piece of equipment, from lighting and ventilation systems to pruning shears and pH meters, has a distinct function in the overall operation. Growers may create a thriving production environment, maintain plant health, and eventually accomplish successful and gratifying cannabis growing by making the necessary investments in equipment and using the relevant tools.

Setting up a grow space

In order to successfully cultivate cannabis, one of the most important steps is to set up an ideal growing space. In order to provide the optimal climate for healthy plant growth and to maximize harvests, the right setup plays an essential role, and this is true regardless of whether you intend to conduct your operation indoors or in a greenhouse.

The selection of an acceptable location is the first stage in the process of building up a grow space. When selecting a location for your grow space, keep the following considerations in mind:

Determine the amount of space that is available, taking into account the total number of plants that you intend to grow. Make sure the area has enough space for the plants to flourish, suitable lighting installations, and easy access for any maintenance tasks that need to be performed.

Pick a location that has adequate ventilation and airflow throughout the area. A healthy amount of air exchange contributes to the maintenance of ideal levels of temperature, humidity, and carbon dioxide (CO2), hence preventing the accumulation of musty air, mold, or pests.

If you plan to cultivate plants indoors, you should look for a place that provides convenient access to energy and allows you to set up lighting and ventilation systems without any trouble. Make sure that the space can meet the power requirements of the lighting system you've chosen.

It is possible that the organization and design of your grow space will have a significant impact on the effectiveness and output of your production. When planning the layout, be sure to take into account the following aspects:

It is important to leave adequate space between plants in order to facilitate healthy air circulation and light penetration. Plants that are grown in close proximity to one another might cause increased levels of humidity, pest infestations, and decreased yields.

Establishing paths in between the plant rows will make it much simpler to perform routine maintenance activities such as watering, pruning, and monitoring. Make sure there is enough space to move around and tend to the plants without causing any harm to them.

Maintaining the plants, mixing the nutrients, and storing the equipment should all be done in a specific part of the grow space that is designated as the work area. Increasing productivity and streamlining the growing process can be accomplished by better organizing your tools and supplies in this area.

Think about protecting your grow space by putting in place some security precautions. Among these measures are the securing of access points, the installation of monitoring systems, and the use of lockable cabinets to store expensive equipment and supplies.

Lighting is an essential element that must be present in any indoor grow space. When putting in place your lighting and electrical systems, take into consideration the following aspects:

Your growth objectives, financial constraints, and available space should all factor into your decision on the lighting system you choose. There is also the possibility of using fluorescent lighting, light-emitting diodes (LEDs), or high-intensity discharge (HID) lights. Metal halide or high-pressure sodium are both examples of HID lights. In terms of energy efficiency, heat production, and spectrum modification, each one has a set of benefits and considerations that are unique to itself.

Ensure that there is an even distribution of light throughout the canopy by positioning the lights in such a way that this is possible. As the plants get larger, you'll need to adjust the height and angle of the lights so that they continue to provide the ideal amount of light and retain adequate coverage.

Check that your home's electrical system is capable of supplying the power needs of the lighting configuration you've chosen. It is recommended that you seek the advice of an experienced electrician to see whether or not the grow area requires any modifications to the electrical system or the installation of additional circuits.

Installing timers to automate the light cycles will ensure that the photoperiods for both the vegetative and flowering stages are uniform and accurate. This helps plants respond more like they would to natural sunlight, which regulates their development and flowering.

Maintaining a healthy grow space requires careful attention to both the ventilation and environmental conditions of the space. When putting in place systems for environmental management and ventilation, you should take into consideration the following aspects:

Installing exhaust fans in the grow space will help to remove stale air, excess heat, and excess humidity. Intake fans are responsible for bringing in new air and helping to enhance air exchange. Make sure the fans are the right size for the grow space by measuring the volume of the space they are in.

Installing carbon filters in the exhaust system will eliminate odors and prevent the powerful cannabis fragrances from escaping the grow space. This is of utmost significance for the sake of protecting one's privacy and abiding by the rules established by the law.

In order to keep the conditions for plant growth at their optimum level, temperature and humidity controllers should be utilized. Depending on the exact requirements of your production system, this may involve the use of air conditioners, heaters, dehumidifiers, or humidifiers.

During the stage of vegetative growth, you may want to give some thought to increase the levels of carbon dioxide (CO_2) in the grow space. In order to raise CO_2 levels, one can make use of CO_2 generators or tanks; however, monitoring and control mechanisms are required in order to avoid reaching unsafely high levels.

For the sake of the plant's health and a timely supply of nutrients, it is vital to choose an adequate growing medium and to set up an effective irrigation system. When preparing the growing medium and the watering, make sure to take into consideration the following aspects:

Determine how you will be cultivating the plant, as well as your personal preferences, before selecting an appropriate growing medium. There are a variety of growing mediums available, including soil, soilless mixtures (such coco coir or peat moss), and hydroponic systems. In terms of nutrient delivery, water retention, and pH stability, each has particular requirements and considerations that must be met.

Install an irrigation system that will supply the plants with nutrients in a manner that is both consistent and accurate. Drip systems, flood and drain systems, and aeroponic systems are some of the available alternatives. When trying to maximize the health and development of plants, it is important to take into account a variety of elements, including the concentration of the nutrient solution, the levels of pH, and the frequency of irrigation.

Make sure there is adequate drainage in the grow space by choosing containers that have drainage holes in them or by building a sloped floor. This minimizes waterlogging and makes it possible to collect excess water and nutrient runoff, both of which can then be disposed of in an appropriate manner.

Think about making use of monitoring systems and automation technologies in order to monitor and manage environmental factors like pH, nutrient levels, and moisture content. These systems can help maintain optimal growing conditions and provide real-time data that can be adjusted and fine-tuned for optimal results.

In conclusion, establishing a grow space needs meticulous planning, close attention to detail, and consideration of a wide range of aspects in order to produce an atmosphere that is conducive to the successful production of cannabis. Every aspect of your cultivation attempts, from choosing the right location to putting in place systems for lighting, ventilation, irrigation, and environmental management, has a significant part in determining whether or not you will be successful. By adhering to these rules and adjusting them to your individual requirements, you will be able to create a thriving grow space that encourages the growth of healthy plants, increases yields, and paves the way for you to embark on a road of successful cannabis growing.

CHAPTER
III
Stages of Germination
and Seedlings

Selecting quality cannabis seeds

The selection of high-quality cannabis seeds is the first step in a successful cannabis cultivation journey. The success and productivity of the entire cultivation process depend on the genetic potential and general health of the seeds.

The healthful growth and bountiful yields of the plants depend on the quality of the cannabis seeds. When determining seed quality, take into account the following indicators:

Quality cannabis seeds have a shiny, black exterior. Avoid seeds that are pale in color, cracked, broken, or exhibit symptoms of pests or mold. The seeds' appearance indicates their maturation and possible viability.

Larger and heavier seeds are often more mature and have a better likelihood of germination. Avoid seeds that are too little or light, as they can be immature or have a lower chance of growing into healthy plants.

You may determine the seeds' quality by lightly squeezing them between your fingertips. Good seeds should feel solid and sturdy to the touch. Avoid seeds that feel mushy, spongy, or fragile because they may not germinate as well or may be more prone to damage.

Look into the reputation and genetics of the seed strains you plan to purchase. Reputable breeders and seed banks give comprehensive details on the genetics, strain characteristics, and culture needs of their products. Look for genetic stability, desirable characteristics, and endorsements from other producers.

Cannabis seeds from reliable suppliers are of high quality, authentic, and satisfy customers. When selecting cannabis seeds, keep the following sources in mind:

A vast range of cannabis seeds are collected, stored, and distributed by businesses known as seed banks. Reputable seed banks obtain their seeds from trustworthy breeders and offer thorough details on the genetics, traits, and cultivation advice of each strain. Seek out seed banks with a reputation for excellence and satisfied customers.

Direct sales of seeds to customers are made by some breeders and seed companies. Research breeders having a track record for creating stable genetics and high-quality seeds. Buying directly from breeders can guarantee the authenticity and quality of the seeds.

Participating in online forums and communities dedicated to cultivation of cannabis might yield insightful advice and suggestions for reliable seed suppliers. Growing experts frequently share their insights and advice, which can help you find reliable suppliers and stay away from scams or poor-quality seeds.

Local dispensaries in areas where cannabis production is permitted might stock a range of trustworthy breeders' or seed banks' quality seeds. Consult educated staff members who can direct you toward dependable choices that will serve your cultivation objectives.

Take into account your personal preferences and unique cultivation objectives while choosing cannabis seeds. Take into consideration the following:

Choose the particular qualities, like as aroma, flavor, strength, and effects, that you want in your cannabis plants. You may adapt your cultivation to your desired experience because different strains offer distinctive combinations of these characteristics.

Take into account the environment in your growing space, including the temperature, humidity, and light levels. Pick seeds that will grow well in your region's climate or in the controlled environment of your indoor grow space.

While some strains may be more suited for inexperienced growers, others may call for greater skill and knowledge. To ensure a successful cultivation journey, evaluate your degree of competence and choose seeds that are compatible with your proficiency level.

Analyze each strain's potential yield and flowering period. While some strains have shorter flowering durations and produce lesser yields, others may have longer flowering times and higher yields. Choose seeds that will give you the yield and timing you want.

In conclusion, choosing high-quality cannabis seeds is an essential stage in the production of cannabis. Growers can position themselves for a satisfying and fruitful cultivation journey by taking into account signs of seed quality, conducting reliable source research, and matching seed selections with growth goals. The genetic potential and general condition of the seeds have a big impact on how the cultivation process turns out. Growers can maximize the potential of their cannabis garden and open the door to prosperous and bountiful crops by making thoughtful selections and well-informed decisions.

Germination methods

The beginning of a plant's life cycle, known as germination, is an important stage in the cultivation of cannabis. A thriving cannabis garden is ultimately built on the foundation of healthy growth and vigorous root development.

The process of germination turns a seed into a seedling that is prepared to sprout and grow into a young plant. For successful growing, it is essential to comprehend the basic principles of germination:

Moisture is necessary for seeds to begin germination. A sufficient amount of moisture softens the seed coat, allowing the embryo inside to show itself and begin to grow.

Germination requires ideal temperature conditions. In order to promote germination, cannabis seeds typically need a temperature range of 70-85°F (21-29°C). Enzymatic activity and other metabolic processes required for seedling development are stimulated by warmth.

When germination is taking place, most cannabis seeds prefer a dark atmosphere. Poor seedling development and germination might result from exposure to light.

Growers can choose from a number of germination techniques, each with their own benefits and considerations. Examine the germination techniques listed below:

In direct planting, the seeds are sown directly into the growing medium of choice, such as soil or a soilless mixture. Simply insert the seed into a tiny hole that is only half an inch deep. Put a little layer of growing material over it, then slowly water it. The delicate seedlings can be handled as little as possible using this procedure, but moisture levels must be carefully monitored to avoid either overwatering or underwatering.

The paper towel method is a well-liked germination technique since it is easy and simple to follow. Place the seeds, making sure they are evenly spaced apart and not touching, between wet paper towels or cotton pads. To produce a humid environment, place the moistened seeds in a closed plastic bag or container. Regularly check for germination signals, and once the taproot appears, carefully transfer the seeds to the preferred growing medium.

Pre-soaking is the practice of soaking seeds in water before sowing. The seeds should soak for 12 to 24 hours in a container of room-temperature water. By doing so, the seed coat is softer and the germination process is sped up. Transfer the seeds to the growing medium after pre-soaking so they can continue to germinate.

Peat pellets or germination cubes offer a handy and controlled environment for seedling growth. When moistened, these tiny, compacted components expand and produce a stable, sterile environment for germination. After planting the seeds in the pre-wetted cubes or pellets, the seedlings can be moved into larger pots or straight into the garden after establishing strong roots.

Regardless of the germination technique selected, the following best practices help seedlings germinate and grow successfully:

Start with cannabis seeds of the highest quality from reliable sources. To increase the likelihood of germination, make sure they are healthy, viable, and stored properly.

During germination, keep the right moisture levels. Avoid underwatering, which can impede germination and seedling development, as well as overwatering, which can result in seed rot or fungus problems.

Keep the temperature in the germination-friendly range on a regular basis. To ensure consistent warmth, think about utilizing a propagator or heating mat. Additionally, make sure the area is calm and dark so that germination can proceed unhindered.

Be patient as the germination process unfolds because different strains may take different amounts of time. Check the seeds frequently for germination indicators like the appearance of a taproot or cracks in the seed coat.

To prevent damage, handle germinating seeds and sprouting seedlings gently. To minimize disturbances and avoid damaging fragile roots and growing shoots, use tweezers or clean fingers.

The seedlings are prepared for transplanting into larger containers or into the garden once they have grown sturdy roots and their first set of genuine leaves. Make sure the transplant location's growing medium is ready and create a stable environment for further growth.

In conclusion, germination is a critical stage in the cultivation of cannabis, laying the groundwork for optimal plant growth. Growers may assure ideal seedling establishment and healthy growth by being aware of the basics of germination, studying different germination techniques, and adhering to best practices. Each approach has its own benefits and considerations, whether you decide to use germination cubes, the paper towel method, direct planting, or pre-soaking. Growers can open the door to effective cannabis growing and lay the groundwork for a flourishing garden by choosing the best germination technique and applying best practices.

Transplanting seedlings

An important step in the cultivation of cannabis plants is transplanting seedlings. Young seedlings are transferred during this procedure from their germination containers to larger pots or straight into the garden soil. Transplanting gives seedlings the space, nutrition, and ideal growing conditions they need for strong growth, good root development, and general success in the cannabis garden.

For the health and development of seedlings, successful transplantation is crucial. A number of advantages that transplanting provides help cannabis plants grow successfully include:

Planting seedlings into bigger pots or garden beds gives them plenty of space for their roots to spread out. This encourages the growth of a strong, healthy root system, which helps the plants absorb nutrients and water more effectively. With enough room, the roots can expand unrestrictedly and lay a solid foundation for the plant's general stability and growth.

A plentiful source of nutrients is made available to seedlings by transplanting them into new growing medium or garden soil. Over time, the initial germination medium's nutritional concentration can get reduced. Growers may guarantee that the seedlings have access to a fresh supply of vital nutrients by transplanting, which will help them thrive and experience their best growth.

Seedlings can gradually adapt to the conditions of their final growing environment by being transplanted. The seedlings are subjected to variations in air flow, temperature, and light intensity during this process. Gradual acclimation aids in the development of the plants' tolerance and resilience to their environment, lowering the possibility of transplant shock and promoting long-term growth.

Plant competition for resources like light, water, and nutrients is reduced when seedlings are transplanted into individual pots or evenly spaced garden beds. Without interference from surrounding plants, each seedling may establish its root system. Additionally, the process of transplanting gives growers the chance to examine the seedlings for any indications of pests or illnesses, allowing them to treat possible problems early on and prevent their spread.

Growers should take into account the following criteria to ensure successful transplanting:

Transplant seedlings once they have grown their first true set of leaves and a solid root system. This shows that the seedlings are prepared to withstand the strain of transplanting and acclimate to their new surroundings. Adequate preparation include having the garden beds or transplanting containers ready in advance, making sure they are clean, and filling them with a growing medium suitable for growing cannabis.

For the seedlings to experience the least amount of stress and have the best chance of establishing themselves, proper transplanting methods are crucial. Remove the seedlings from their original containers with care, being mindful not to damage the roots. To ensure that the seedlings sit at the same depth as they did in their original pots, create planting holes in the garden beds or transplanting containers that are the proper size. After transplanting, water the seedlings thoroughly to let the soil settle, and then gently press the growing medium around them.

For transplanted seedlings to continue growing and developing, post-transplant care is essential. If moving from indoor to outdoor cultivation, give the seedlings the right quantity of light and gradually expose them to direct sunlight. Keep an eye on the soil's moisture levels and give the seedlings regular waterings to keep the soil moist without becoming soggy. Consider elements like the location and the particular needs of the cannabis strain being grown when adjusting the frequency of watering. Use the proper precautions, like as shading, row coverings, or organic pest management techniques, to protect the seedlings from harsh weather, pests, and illnesses.

In conclusion, transplanting seedlings is an essential step in growing cannabis plants that are strong and thriving. Growers can set the groundwork for effective growth and overall plant health by providing enough room for root development, availability to new nutrients, and gradual adaptability to the growing environment. For the seedlings to experience the least amount of stress and to have the best chance of establishing themselves, it is crucial to use the right timing, preparation, transplanting methods, and post-transplant care. Transplanted seedlings will thrive with care and attention to detail, laying the groundwork for a flourishing cannabis garden and a bountiful harvest.

Caring for seedlings

The tender, tiny plants known as seedlings contain the potential of a fruitful cannabis garden. In the critical phase of cannabis production known as seedling care, producers offer the nurturing environment and care needed for optimal growth and development.

A key component of cannabis growing that lays the groundwork for healthy growth is the care of seedlings. In order to preserve their health and vigor, seedlings need extra care and attention because they are at their most vulnerable stage. Healthy growth, prevent possible problems, and a smooth transition from seedlings to adult plants are all supported by good care techniques.

The proper temperature and lighting conditions are an essential part of seedling care. In order to enable photosynthesis and wholesome growth, seedlings require enough light. A light source that resembles natural sunlight can be produced using full-spectrum fluorescent or LED grow lamps. The best growth and stress prevention are achieved by maintaining the proper temperature range of 70-80°F (21-27°C) during the day and slightly colder temps at night.

The wellbeing and development of seedlings depend on proper nutrition management and irrigation. Providing adequate moisture without overwatering or underwatering is a need of proper watering techniques. Before watering, the growing medium's top inch should be dry. Additionally, the cotyledon leaves and the stored energy in the seed are the first sources of nutrition for seedlings. As they expand, extra nutrients are required to promote their development. Their nutritional requirements can be met by gradually applying a mild, balanced nutrient solution or a seedling fertilizer.

During the seedling stage, it is essential to prevent pests and illnesses. The first line of protection is to keep the surroundings clean and sterile. Infestations can be avoided by implementing integrated pest management techniques, which include routine inspection, the introduction of beneficial insects, and the use of organic pest control techniques. The risk of fungi illnesses like damping-off is minimized by good airflow and effective moisture management.

The act of transplanting is an essential part of seedling care. Prior to being transplanted, seedlings must have grown a robust root system and their first set of true leaves, thus timing is crucial. The success of the seedlings' establishment depends on carefully removing them from their original pots and giving them a suitable growing medium or garden bed. In order to support their recovery and ongoing growth, post-transplant care include supplying enough moisture, light, and environmental conditions.

In conclusion, seedling care is an essential part of cannabis growing that paves the way for strong growth and fruitful plant development.

Growers may protect the health of their seedlings by providing the proper lighting, temperature, hydration, nutrition management, taking precautions against pests and diseases, and using the proper transplanting methods. A lively and flourishing cannabis garden will result from giving seedlings careful attention and care. Growers provide the conditions for a fruitful cultivation process and abundant harvest by taking care of the seedlings.

CHAPTER
IV
Stage of the Vegetation

Providing the right light conditions

The growth and development of cannabis plants depend heavily on light. They are photosynthesis-dependent organisms that use light energy to power the process of photosynthesis, which supports their development, productivity, and overall well-being. Creating the ideal lighting conditions is essential for cannabis production success.

It is impossible to overstate how important light is to cannabis plants. Light has a significant impact on a variety of physiological processes that support healthy plant growth, impacting their growth and development.

The primary mechanism by which plants transform light energy into chemical energy and use it to create oxygen and glucose is known as photosynthesis. This mechanism provides the energy that cannabis plants require for development and growth. Photosynthesis may only occur under certain lighting conditions, which limits plant growth and production potential.

Different light spectra have varying effects on the growth and development of cannabis plants. Blue light with a wavelength between 400 and 500 nm is necessary for vegetative growth. It encourages dense, bushy growth as well as the growth of robust foliage. Blue light is essential for controlling stomatal control, leaf growth, and the production of proteins required for photosynthesis. The flowering and fruiting stages require red light, which has a wavelength between 600 and 700 nm. It promotes bud formation, increases resin production, and stimulates the release of hormones that regulate flowering. Red light is also necessary for stem growth and elongation. Blue and red light are balancedly combined in full-spectrum light, which covers the whole spectrum of visible light. Throughout the whole growth cycle, it promotes the general health and development of the plant.

Growers also need to think about the light strength and duration in addition to the various light spectrum. The amount of light energy that reaches a plant's surface is referred to as the light intensity. To sustain photosynthesis and good growth, cannabis plants need sufficient light intensity. The plant's stage of growth determines the optimum light intensity. Light levels between 1,000 and 2,500 foot-candles (or 10,000 to 25,000 lux) are advised during the vegetative stage. This range encourages rapid growth and the development of leaves. To enhance bud development and resin production during the flowering stage, higher light levels between 25,000 and 50,000 lux (or 2,500 to 5,000 foot-candles) are required.

Another important aspect is light duration, or the amount of hours of light a plant receives each day. Cannabis plants grow with longer periods of light, usually 18 to 24 hours a day, during the vegetative stage. This prolonged period of light encourages vegetative growth and supplies the energy required for the establishment of lush foliage. The shift to flowering is triggered when the light duration is reduced to 12 hours of light and 12 hours of continuous darkness. This light schedule stimulates the plant to concentrate its energy on bud growth by simulating the fluctuations in natural light duration that occur during the fall season.

To offer the required lighting conditions for cannabis production, growers have the option of using artificial lighting. Cannabis has traditionally been grown indoors using high-intensity discharge (HID) illumination, such as metal halide (MH) and high-pressure sodium (HPS) lamps. While HPS lamps emit a red spectrum that is perfect for flowering, MH lamps emit a blue spectrum that is suitable for the vegetative stage. HID lighting is appropriate for larger growing spaces because of its high light intensity and coverage. To maintain ideal temperatures, they must be properly ventilated because they produce a lot of heat.

Light-Emitting Diode (LED) lighting, which has grown in popularity recently, is an additional lighting alternative. Energy efficiency, a longer lifespan, and the flexibility to alter the light spectrum are just a few benefits of LED lighting. Growers may tailor their lighting system by adjusting LED lights to produce the precise spectra needed at different growth stages. Additionally, because they produce less heat, they may be grown either indoors or in smaller growing spaces without the need for large cooling systems.

Compact fluorescent lamps (CFLs) and T5 fluorescent tubes are two types of fluorescent lighting that are an affordable alternative for small-scale or low-intensity lighting requirements. They produce less light than HID or LED lights but may still be appropriate for seedlings, clones, or small vegetative setups.

For maintaining the optimum light intensity without harming the plants, proper light distances and hanging heights are essential. The best hanging height will vary depending on the type of lighting, how bright it is, and the stage of plant growth. The manufacturer's guidelines should be followed by growers while adjusting the hanging height. This reduces the possibility of shade and encourages balanced growth by ensuring that the light is distributed equally across the canopy.

In conclusion, it is essential to create the ideal lighting conditions for cannabis production. The process of photosynthesis is powered by light, which also fuels the growth and development of plants. Growers can maximize their cultivation efforts by comprehending the importance of light, the function of various light spectra, considerations for light intensity and duration, and the usage of artificial lighting. Growers may unleash the full potential of their cannabis plants and promote healthy development, abundant yields, and high-quality harvests by creating the optimum lighting conditions. Growers can brighten the way to productive cannabis production with the correct lighting.

Nutrients and fertilizers for healthy growth

For cannabis plants to grow and develop healthily, nutrients and fertilizers are essential. By giving plants the ideal ratio of vital nutrients, you can make sure they have the building blocks they need for healthy growth, vibrant foliage, and abundant yields.

The basic elements that plants require to perform important tasks and develop are provided by nutrients, which are the lifeblood of plants. For optimal growth and development, cannabis plants, like all other plants, need a balanced supply of macronutrients and micronutrients.

Macronutrients are essential for plant development, structure, and overall health and are needed in greater amounts. Nitrogen (N), phosphorus (P), potassium (K), calcium (Ca), magnesium (Mg), and sulfur (S) are the macronutrients required by cannabis plants. Every macronutrient has a specific impact on different elements of plant growth. Nitrogen is essential for leaf growth and healthy foliage. For plants to develop their roots, flower, and bear fruit, phosphorus is required. Potassium supports bud growth, disease resistance, and overall plant vitality. Both calcium and magnesium support enzyme functions and cell structure. Protein synthesis and the synthesis of chlorophyll both involve sulfur.

Cannabis plants also need micronutrients, which are equally important for good growth but are required in smaller amounts than macronutrients. Iron (Fe), manganese (Mn), zinc (Zn), copper (Cu), boron (B), molybdenum (Mo), and chlorine (Cl) are examples of micronutrients. These micronutrients play a role in photosynthesis, enzymatic reactions, and overall metabolic processes.

To guarantee that plants receive the proper balance of nutrients, effective nutrient management is essential. Both nutrient surpluses and deficits can harm the health and development of plants. Visual signs of nutrient deficits include leaf yellowing or discoloration, slowed development, or necrosis. Because each nutrient shortage manifests differently, growers can recognize and correct the individual nutrient imbalances. For prompt intervention and correction, regular monitoring and identification of nutrient deficiencies are necessary.

However, too much of a certain nutrient can also be detrimental to the health of plants. Nutrient imbalances and toxicity brought on by excessive fertilization might impede plant growth. Nutrient lockout, which happens when too many nutrients are present and make some nutrients unavailable to the plant, might cause subsequent nutrient deficits. It is essential to adhere to dosage recommendations and carefully watch plants for symptoms of nutrient burn or toxicity in order to prevent nutrient excesses.

In order to improve nutritional levels, growers might select between organic and synthetic fertilizers. Organic fertilizers come from organic materials like fish emulsion, compost, manure, or bone meal.

They support the health of the soil and microbial activity by gradually releasing nutrients over time. Organic fertilizers enhance soil structure and nutrient retention, encouraging environmentally friendly farming methods. However, compared to synthetic fertilizers, they might have lesser nutritional contents.

Chemical formulas are used to create synthetic fertilizers, often known as inorganic or chemical fertilizers, which deliver particular nutritional ratios. They work quickly and are easily accessible. Synthetic fertilizers are appropriate for hydroponic or soilless growing systems because they give growers precise control over nutrient levels. However, if synthetic fertilizers are used carelessly, they might cause nutrient imbalances, environmental issues, or deterioration of soil health.

It is essential to create a nutrient schedule to ensure a steady and balanced supply of nutrients throughout the growth cycle. Cannabis plants need more nitrogen during the vegetative stage to maintain their robust leaf and stem growth. During this phase, a nutritional solution with a greater nitrogen-to-phosphorus ratio is acceptable. For the production of chlorophyll and the general health of plants, micronutrients like iron and manganese are also crucial.

Plants' nutritional needs change as they enter the flowering stage. When it comes to promoting flowers development and resin synthesis, phosphorus and potassium become even more important. At this stage, the nutrient solution should be altered to have a higher phosphorus-to-nitrogen ratio. For appropriate food absorption and enzymatic activities, adequate quantities of calcium and magnesium are additionally necessary.

Many growers use a flushing period at the end of the flowering phase. To wash out any surplus nutrients and enhance the quality of the final crop, plants are watered with pure water that is devoid of nutrients or fertilizers.

For nutrient availability and uptake, the growing medium must be kept within the optimum pH range. Generally speaking, cannabis plants prefer a pH range of 5.8 to 6.5 that is somewhat acidic. The pH of fertilizer solutions or soil should be regularly monitored and adjusted to achieve effective nutrient uptake.

In conclusion, fertilizers and nutrients are essential for the proper growth and development of cannabis plants. Growers can maximize plant health, vigor, and yields by giving the proper ratio of critical macronutrients and micronutrients. Maintaining good nutrient management necessitates taking into account nutrient excesses and deficiencies as well as choosing between organic and synthetic fertilizers. The best plant growth is supported by creating nutrient regimens that are specific to the various growth stages. Growers can fuel their cannabis plants for optimum health and success with correct fertilizer management, creating the conditions for a plentiful and high-quality harvest.

Watering and maintaining proper humidity

Growing cannabis requires careful attention to humidity control and watering. Water is essential to a plant's survival because it makes nutrient intake, photosynthesis, and other metabolic processes possible. Humidity, meantime, has an impact on transpiration, water loss, and the plant's capacity to control moisture and temperature.

Water is a vital resource that directly affects the health and development of plants. Watering methods that are appropriate give plants the moisture they need to perform essential physiological functions. Water serves as a medium through which nutrients are absorbed by the roots of plants during nutrient uptake. Water serves as a conduit, carrying vital components from the growing medium to different areas of the plant and promoting growth, metabolism, and general wellness. Water is also essential for the photosynthesis process, which is how plants turn light energy into chemical energy. Water molecules split during photosynthesis, producing oxygen as a byproduct and hydrogen atoms for the synthesis of carbohydrates.

Another important function that is aided by water is transpiration. Through tiny openings on the plant's leaves known as stomata, water vapor is released. Temperature regulation, turgidity maintenance, and nutrient transfer are all aided by transpiration. An adequate watering schedule ensures that there is enough water available for transpiration, which supports healthy plant activity.

The size of the plant, the growing medium, the environment, and other variables all affect how frequently and how to water a plant. Compared to mature plants, younger plants like seedlings or clones have smaller root systems and need less water. To prevent overwatering, seedlings and clones may benefit from more frequent but lighter watering. Watering schedules can be changed as plants mature and expand to accommodate their increasing water requirements.

The kind of growing medium utilized affects how much water is needed. In addition to retaining moisture, well-drained soils allow extra water to drain away. Due to their increased drainage rates, soilless mediums like coco coir or hydroponic systems may need to be watered more frequently. To avoid under- or overwatering, it is essential to keep an eye on the moisture levels in the growing medium.

Environmental factors also affect the amount of water needed. Plant transpiration rates increase with higher temperatures and lower humidity levels, which causes rapid water loss. To avoid moisture stress under these circumstances, more frequent watering or modifications to watering methods may be required. Techniques for watering can also be changed to ensure efficient water distribution and reduce water waste. Techniques like drip irrigation systems or bottom watering offer focused watering while lowering the possibility of overwatering.

For the successful production of cannabis, humidity levels are crucial. The level of air moisture is referred to as humidity. Plant transpiration rates, nutrient uptake, and general plant health are all impacted by the right humidity conditions. High humidity slows transpiration, which causes the plant to lose water more gradually. On the other hand, low humidity speeds up perspiration, which can increase water demand and perhaps cause moisture stress.

The availability and uptake of nutrients by plants are also impacted by humidity. Due to slower transport of nutrients in the growing medium and less evaporation, high humidity levels might hinder nutrient absorption. To achieve maximum nutrient uptake and availability for healthy plant growth, correct humidity levels must be maintained.

Controlling humidity is essential for preventing the development and spread of fungi illnesses. Poor air circulation and high humidity combine to generate ideal circumstances for the growth of fungi, potentially resulting in crop loss. By limiting the development of stagnant air, adequate ventilation and air circulation assist in controlling humidity levels. The ventilation and humidity in the growth space are improved by exhaust fans, intake vents, and oscillating fans. Stronger plant stems result from proper air circulation, which also aids in preventing the growth of mold or mildew.

Regular monitoring with a hygrometer is essential to maintaining the right amounts of humidity. Depending on the stage of growth, different humidity ranges are ideal. Humidity values between 40% and 70% are often advised during the vegetative period. To limit the risk of fungal illnesses during the flowering period, humidity should be gradually decreased to a range of 40% to 50%.

Dehumidifiers can be used to remove extra moisture from the air in environments with high humidity, helping to regulate humidity levels and preventing the growth of mold or mildew. In contrast, low humidity areas can benefit from the use of humidifiers or misting systems to maintain ideal conditions by raising moisture levels.

Another method for controlling humidity levels is to water at the proper time of day. It is best to water plants during the day's cooler times, such as the mornings or evenings, so that any excess moisture can be allowed to evaporate before the temperatures rise. This procedure aids in avoiding persistently high humidity levels that may cause problems with moisture.

In conclusion, keeping the right humidity levels and watering your plants regularly are important aspects of growing cannabis. Water is a necessary resource that promotes photosynthesis, nutrient uptake, and general plant health. Plant transpiration rates, nutrient uptake, and the avoidance of fungi infections are all influenced by humidity levels. Growers may maximize plant health and achieve effective cannabis production by comprehending the significance of watering, taking into account considerations for watering frequency and approaches, knowing the role of humidity, and putting plans in place to maintain optimal humidity levels. Growers can guarantee that their cannabis plants receive the essential hydration, maintain appropriate transpiration rates, and flourish toward a plentiful and high-quality harvest by using proper watering and humidity management.

Pruning and training techniques

In order to shape plants, enhance light penetration and airflow, and increase yields, pruning and training procedures are crucial practices in cannabis growing. To optimize plant structure, improve bud development, and advance overall plant health, these procedures involve the selective removal or manipulation of plant growth.

Cannabis growers have access to useful resources like pruning and training methods that have a number of advantages for the growth and production of plants. First of all, these methods enhance light penetration. Cannabis plants naturally have a propensity to grow a thick canopy, which may prevent light from reaching lower foliage and bud sites. Growers can make sure that light reaches more parts of the plant by carefully eliminating extra foliage and widening the canopy. Increased photosynthesis, better bud development, and higher yields are all results of improved light penetration.

Second, pruning and training methods improve airflow and aid in avoiding problems caused with high humidity and poor air circulation. The likelihood of mold, mildew, and pest infestations might increase when there is dense foliage because it can foster an atmosphere with high humidity and stagnant air. Growers can improve airflow within the plant canopy, lowering humidity levels and limiting the development of moisture, by selectively removing or bending branches. Additionally, improved airflow makes it more difficult for pests to colonize the plant, encouraging better development.

Additionally, growers can re-shape the structure of the plant through training and pruning to improve support and growth dispersion. Plants can create a more uniform and sturdy structure by pruning weak or superfluous branches and encouraging upward growth. This encourages stronger development and makes maintenance activities like feeding, watering, and insect control easier to reach. The likelihood of branches breaking under the weight of buds during the flowering stage is also decreased by a well-shaped plant structure.

Additionally, pruning and training methods maximize yields. Growers can direct the plant's energy toward creating bigger, better-quality buds by controlling the rate of plant development. Using pruning procedures, lower, shaded foliage that wouldn't considerably increase yield is removed. This enables the plant to concentrate its energy on producing bigger, more powerful buds. Increased yields are the result of training methods like topping or bending branches that promote the growth of many bud sites.

Depending on the plant's growth stage and the intended plant structure, a variety of pruning techniques can be used. A common approach is called FIMming, which avoids cutting the apical meristem totally by only removing a portion of it. By using this method, more potential bud sites are created and several new shoots are encouraged to grow. Another frequent pruning technique is topping, which involves cutting off the apical meristem of the main stem to encourage the development of two or more new shoots. This method promotes lateral development and results in a bushier, multi-cola plant.

Techniques for training plants can help to further optimize plant growth in addition to pruning. Bending or tying down branches as part of low-stress training (LST) results in a more horizontal growth pattern. Growers can enhance light penetration and create an equal canopy by gently bending the branches outward from the center of the plant. LST lowers the danger of mold and mildew by promoting more uniform bud development and greater airflow throughout the plant.

The Screen of Green (SCROG) method of training is another well-liked method. It entails supporting the plant's development and directing it to grow horizontally using a screen or net. As the plant develops, the screen's branches are intertwined to form an even canopy and encourage more bud sites. SCROG increases light exposure and uniformizes plant structure, increasing yields.

It is important to keep in mind a few things when using pruning and training strategies. To start, timing is important. The vegetative stage is the greatest time to use pruning and training procedures since plants can recover and redirect their growth during this time. Before moving into the flowering stage, it's crucial to give plants time to recover and develop new growth.

Second, the plant's overall health is crucial. Techniques for training or pruning weak or stressed plants may not be appropriate. Examining the plant's general health and vitality is crucial before making any major alterations. Pruning and training are more likely to provide favorable results in healthy plants, which leads to improved growth and development.

Another crucial factor is sterilization. When making pruning cuts, it is best to use clean, sterile equipment to reduce the possibility of spreading germs or diseases to the plant. Rubbing alcohol or another disinfectant should be used to sterilize pruning tools between cuts to avoid cross-contamination.

Finally, patience is the key. Techniques for pruning and training involve patience and careful attention. Monitoring the plant's reaction to the strategies used is crucial, and any necessary adjustments should be made. It is important to pay close attention and base judgments on the specific requirements of each plant because they may respond differently.

The use of pruning and training procedures, which enable growers to shape plants for the best development, highest yields, and general plant health, is a crucial practice in the production of cannabis. These methods boost ventilation, increase light penetration, and encourage the growth of numerous bud sites. Growers may shape their cannabis plants to produce a lot of high-quality yields by knowing the value of pruning and training, as well as various techniques including topping, LST, and SCROG. Cannabis growers may regulate plant structure and maximize growth for a fruitful and satisfying experience by using the right pruning and training procedures.

CHAPTER
V
Stage of Flowering

Understanding the flowering cycle

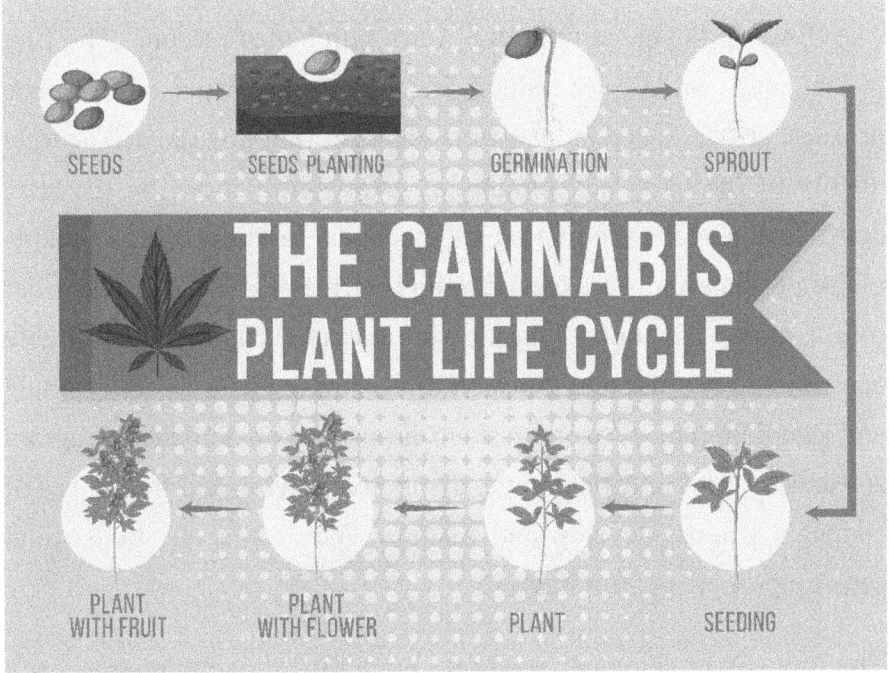

A crucial stage in the cultivation of cannabis is the flowering cycle, during which the plants move from vegetative growth to the development of flowers or buds. It is essential for growers to understand every aspect of the flowering cycle in order to produce the best yields, powerful cannabinoid profiles, and desired scents and flavors.

The ability of the plant to produce flowers and ultimately harvestable buds is determined by the flowering cycle, which is a crucial stage in the development of cannabis. For growers, this stage is crucial since it has a direct bearing on the amount and quality of the finished product. Growers can optimize their cultivation techniques and raise their chances of success by having a thorough understanding of the flowering cycle.

The flowering cycle is important for a number of reasons. The first is that buds, which are valued for their cannabinoid and terpene profiles, are produced by cannabis plants during this stage. The total quality of the harvested product is greatly influenced by the size, density, and resin production of the buds. Additionally, cannabis plants produce and store cannabinoids, such as THC, CBD, and other useful substances, during the flowering cycle. To achieve desirable cannabinoid profiles and potency, this phase must be carefully timed and handled. The flowering stage is also when terpenes, fragrant substances that contribute to the distinctive flavors and fragrances of cannabis strains, develop and mature. They affect the buds' final sensory properties after harvest.

The flowering cycle is divided into numerous separate phases, each of which is distinguished by certain alterations in plant growth. It is crucial to comprehend these stages in order to time cultivation procedures and improve plant care. The transition from vegetative growth to the pre-flowering stage takes place after. Nodes separate at this phase, and female plants exhibit pistils, which are tiny hair-like structures. At the locations of the female pistils, buds start to form and grow in the early stages of flowering. To encourage good bud growth during this phase, nutrient and environmental conditions are essential. Bud growth and size persist during the middle stage of flowering. During this stage, trichome production, which contains important cannabinoids and terpenes, increases. To prevent nutrient deficiency and environmental stress, it is essential to closely monitor nutrient levels, humidity, and temperature. The last development of the buds and the ripening of the trichomes define the late flowering stage. To determine the best time for harvest, growers must closely examine the color of the trichomes and pistils.

The flowering cycle and the general success of cannabis growing are influenced by a number of environmental and cultural factors. The flowering phase is started and maintained in large part by the light cycle. During the vegetative stage of the cannabis plant, the light cycle must be changed from 18 hours of light to 6 hours of darkness to 12 hours of light to 12 hours of darkness. For healthy flower development, a constant and persistent light cycle is essential. The flowering cycle is substantially influenced by temperature and humidity levels. The ideal temperature range for cannabis plants is between 20 and 26 degrees Celsius (68 and 78 degrees Fahrenheit) during the day and a little lower at night.

In order to prevent mold or mildew problems, humidity levels should be regularly monitored and managed. It's critical to control nutrients properly during the flowering cycle. During this stage, cannabis plants require specific nutrients, with a greater need for phosphorus and potassium. By modifying fertilizer formulas and keeping an eye on nutrient levels, deficiencies or excesses that could harm flower development are prevented. Any type of environmental stress, such sharp temperature swings, light leaks, insects or diseases, might interfere with the flowering process and damage the health of the plant. For the best flower development and to avoid losing priceless yields, a steady and stress-free environment is necessary.

To guarantee optimal cannabis cultivation, flowering cycle timing and maintenance are essential. Genetics, desired plant size, and culture objectives can all have an impact on the timing of the transition from vegetative growth to the flowering stage, which is critical. During the flowering period, it's crucial to give the right nutrition and supplements. Healthy bud development is ensured by modifying fertilizer formulations to satisfy the plants' evolving needs, particularly by adding more phosphorus and potassium.

Throughout the flowering period, careful observation of environmental variables like temperature, humidity, and airflow is crucial. By preserving ideal circumstances, one can encourage the development of healthy plants and lower the danger of pests and illnesses. For desired cannabinoid profiles and overall quality, determining the best time to harvest is essential. Considerations should be made for elements like trichome color, pistil maturity, and strain-specific advice.

In conclusion, successful cannabis production depends critically on an understanding of the intricacies of the flowering cycle. The plant's capacity to generate terpenes, cannabinoids, and flowers depends on this crucial stage. Growers can maximize their cultivation operations and produce plentiful, high-quality yields by being aware of the major stages involved, taking into account environmental and cultural factors, and using the right timing and care. Growing cannabis is rewarding and profitable when growers have a thorough understanding of the flowering cycle and can confidently traverse this pivotal period.

Light and darkness requirements

One of the most important aspects in the growth and development of cannabis plants, as well as the final quality and yield of the harvested product, is light. To improve their cultivation techniques and obtain effective results, growers must comprehend the light and darkness requirements of cannabis plants.

Cannabis cultivation depends on the presence of light and darkness, which have an impact on a variety of features of plant growth and development. Light-dark interactions have an impact on photoperiodic reactions, which are essential for inducing particular growth phases in cannabis plants.

Photosynthesis, the process by which plants turn light energy into chemical energy to ultimately power growth and development, depends on light. The energy needed for photosynthesis to produce sugars and other vital molecules is provided by light. Additionally, light affects photomorphogenesis, which is the term for how light affects the morphology, structure, and physiological functions of plants. It has an impact on the architecture of the plant, leaf development, chlorophyll synthesis, and the emergence of secondary metabolites.

For cannabis plants, darkness is equally vital because it enables critical functions like respiration, which helps plants to release carbon dioxide and break down stored energy. Additionally, the release of hormones that control growth, flowering, and other developmental phases is brought on in plants by darkness. Crucial metabolic processes, such as the disintegration of carbohydrates and the production of proteins required for plant growth, take place during the dark period.

The length of light and dark periods within a 24-hour cycle, or photoperiod, is crucial for the growth and development of cannabis. In cannabis plants, particular growth stages are triggered by various photoperiods. An average plant needs between 18 and 24 hours of light every day to be in the vegetative stage. The growth of leaves, branches, and a strong root system are all encouraged by this prolonged photoperiod. In contrast, the shorter photoperiod of 12 hours of light and 12 hours without interruption of darkness is used to start the flowering stage. This shift in photoperiod initiates flowering, which results in the development of flowers or buds.

Light's color and intensity have a big impact on how cannabis grows and develops. The physiology of plants is influenced by specific light wavelengths in different ways. During the vegetative stage, blue light, which has a wavelength of about 400–500 nanometers, is essential because it encourages foliage growth, sturdy stems, and general plant vitality. It modulates phototropism, the plant's reaction to light direction, by promoting the synthesis of chlorophyll.

During the flowering stage, red light, which has a wavelength of about 600–700 nanometers, is extremely important. It improves bud development, encourages the synthesis of secondary metabolites including terpenes and cannabinoids, and affects the release of flowering hormones. The plant's perception of the length of day and night is influenced by far-red light, which has a wavelength of roughly 700–800 nanometers. Since exposure to far-red light during the night can prevent the plant from naturally flowering, it is especially crucial during the flowering stage.

The rate of photosynthesis and overall plant development are influenced by light intensity, which is expressed in terms of photosynthetic photon flux density (PPFD). Maximizing plant health and productivity requires providing the proper light intensity for each stage of growth. Depending on the particular growth stage, strain, and environmental factors, different light intensities are required. Plants obtain the ideal quantity of light for their developmental needs when the light intensity is monitored and altered.

The right lighting environment must be created by carefully taking into account a number of aspects. The choice of light source is crucial; in cannabis growth, LED grow lights, fluorescent lights, and high-intensity discharge (HID) lamps are frequently employed. Each type of light source has advantages and considerations to keep in mind in terms of energy efficiency, light output, and light spectrum.

Each stage of growth should have a constant and suitable duration and schedule of light and darkness. The light schedule can be automated with timers, ensuring the plants get the necessary photoperiod. To prevent light burn or inadequate light intensity, the distance between the light source and the plants should be carefully regulated. The light source's coverage area needs to be large enough to evenly distribute light across all plants. To ensure optimum performance and avoid any problems that can threaten plant health and growth, light sources must be regularly inspected and maintained.

In conclusion, knowing the cannabis plants' needs for light and darkness is crucial for getting optimal cultivation results. Light has a significant impact on plant development, growth, and cannabinoid synthesis. Growers may maximize plant health, production, and desired cannabinoid profiles by knowing the significance of light and darkness, understanding the function of photoperiod, taking into account light spectrum and intensity, and putting optimal lighting methods into practice. Cannabis growers can use the power of light to grow healthy, fruitful, and high-quality cannabis plants by using a well-designed lighting environment.

Managing nutrient ratios

Managing nutrient ratios is an essential part of growing cannabis since it has a direct impact on the health, development, and quality of the plant. In order to achieve desired results, it is crucial to comprehend the function of critical nutrients, their ideal ratios, and how to maintain a balanced nutrient regimen.

Due to the specialized roles that various nutrients play in the growth and health of cannabis plants, managing nutrient ratios is essential for guaranteeing healthy plant development. In order to sustain metabolic processes, facilitate biochemical processes, and act as the building blocks for plant structures, nutrients are crucial. Growers may encourage optimal growth, minimize nutrient deficiencies or toxicities, and improve the plant's capacity to create desirable compounds like cannabinoids and terpenes by maintaining proper nutritional ratios.

A variety of vital nutrients are needed by cannabis plants for proper growth and development. Both macronutrients and micronutrients can be extensively used to describe these nutrients. Macronutrients, such as nitrogen (N), phosphorus (P), potassium (K), calcium (Ca), magnesium (Mg), and sulfur (S), are needed by plants in greater amounts. For leaf development, vegetative growth, and the production of chlorophyll, nitrogen is crucial. Phosphorus encourages the growth of roots, flowers, and the transfer of energy. Potassium helps plants tolerate stress, regulate water use, and maintain overall health.

Involved in cell structure, enzyme activation, and nutrition uptake are the minerals calcium and magnesium. The synthesis of proteins and the general health of plants both depend on sulfur. Even though they are required in smaller levels, micronutrients are crucial for plant growth. Iron (Fe), manganese (Mn), zinc (Zn), copper (Cu), boron (B), molybdenum (Mo), and chlorine (Cl) are some of them. These micronutrients are essential for hormone production, photosynthesis, enzyme activation, and general plant metabolism.

To prevent nutrient deficiencies or toxicities that could impede plant growth and development, adequate nutritional balance must be maintained. When maintaining nutritional ratios, a number of things need to be taken into account. The availability and uptake of nutrients by the plant are substantially influenced by pH levels. For optimum nutrient uptake, cannabis plants normally prefer a pH range of 5.8 to 6.5 that is neutral to slightly acidic. By adjusting pH levels, nutrients are guaranteed to be present in their most soluble forms. Understanding nutrient interactions is crucial because excessive amounts of one nutrient may prevent the uptake of another. Maintaining correct nutritional balance and avoiding imbalances is made possible by monitoring nutrient interactions.

Throughout each stage of growth, cannabis plants have different nutrient needs. In order to stimulate leafy growth, plants need more nitrogen during the vegetative stage. Increased phosphorus and potassium levels are essential for strong flower development and cannabinoid production throughout the flowering stage. Whether organic or synthetic, the source of the nutrients can affect their availability and absorption. While synthetic nutrients are immediately available to the plants, organic nutrients release gradually, supplying a continuous supply over time. Growers should select nutrition sources that suit their preferences and growing objectives.

A number of measures must be used to implement a nutrition management plan effectively. It is essential to start with a high-quality growing medium that has a balanced nutrient composition. An optimal growing environment is created by adding organic matter, compost, or specialized nutrients to the soil or medium. The proper nutrients are given to the plants at the right time by creating a feeding schedule based on the stage of growth. It is possible to take prompt corrective action by monitoring the fertilizer levels in the hydroponic system or growing medium. Nutrient flushing on a regular basis helps keep the balance of nutrients while removing accumulated salts. To correct acute nutrient deficits or increase nutrient uptake effectiveness, supplemental foliar feeding may be applied.

For optimal cannabis development, maximum harvests, and the promotion of the creation of desirable compounds, regulating nutrient ratios is essential. Growers may assure healthy plant development and obtain high-quality harvests by comprehending the essential nutrients that cannabis plants need, taking into account nutrient balancing elements, and putting effective nutrient management tactics into practice. The ability of the plant to create strong cannabinoids and terpenes is supported by maintaining optimal nutrient ratios, which also promote vigorous development and reduce nutrient deficiencies or toxicities. Cultivators can improve plant health, productivity, and the general success of their cannabis cultivation initiatives by using a well-planned nutrition management strategy.

Recognizing and addressing common issues

In order to successfully grow cannabis, one must not only be aware of the ideal growing conditions, but also be able to identify and resolve common problems that may come up during the cultivation process. Growers can maintain plant health, increase yields, and create high-quality cannabis by being aware of potential issues and knowing how to properly treat them.

Cannabis growers frequently deal with pests, which can seriously harm plants if they aren't treated right away. Spider mites, aphids, fungus gnats, and thrips are examples of typical pests that harm cannabis plants. Early response depends on the ability to spot pest infestation symptoms such visible insects, leaf damage, or webbing.

To manage and avoid pests, Integrated Pest Management (IPM) procedures must be used. Regular scouting and monitoring, maintenance of a clean and sanitary growing environment, the use of physical barriers like screens, the introduction of helpful insects for biological control, and the occasional use of organic or chemical treatments are all included in this.

Numerous ailments, including as powdery mildew, botrytis (bud rot), root rot, and fungal infections can affect cannabis plants. These ailments have a negative effect on plant health and decrease yields. Discoloration, wilting, mold growth, or unusual lesions on leaves, stems, or buds are signs of illness.

The first step in disease prevention is to keep the growth environment clean and hygienic. The danger of disease can be reduced with appropriate airflow, sufficient plant spacing, and regular trimming to encourage airflow. Disease can also be avoided by using cannabis strains that are resistant to specific diseases, sterilizing tools and equipment, and using the right irrigation practices to minimize overwatering. In the event of disease, early detection and prompt treatment are crucial. Affected plant material may need to be removed and disposed of, organic or chemical fungicides may be used, and environmental conditions may need to be changed.

The growth, development, and general health of cannabis plants can be dramatically impacted by nutrient deficits. Nitrogen (N), phosphorus (P), potassium (K), magnesium (Mg), iron (Fe), and calcium (Ca) shortages are typical nutrient deficiencies. Depending on the nutrient deficiency, symptoms can include weak stems, stunted growth, or yellowing or browning of the leaves.

In order to address nutrient deficiencies, growers must first pinpoint the precise nutrient the plant is deficient in. Testing in the soil or hydroponic systems can help identify nutrient deficits and levels. Deficiencies can be corrected by modifying nutrient formulations, pH levels, and applying the proper nutrient supplementation or foliar feeding. To avoid nutrient shortages, it's important to regularly analyze your diet and keep up a balanced nutritional routine.

Environmental stressors can have a negative impact on the health and productivity of cannabis plants, such as temperature changes, insufficient humidity levels, high light intensity, or inadequate air circulation. These stressors can cause the plant to develop less slowly, have nutrient imbalances, be more vulnerable to pests and diseases, and generally be weaker.

To reduce environmental stressors, a stable and controlled growing environment is essential. This entails preserving the proper temperature and humidity levels, offering sufficient airflow and ventilation, and using shading or extra lighting as required. The likelihood of stress-related problems is minimized by routinely assessing environmental circumstances and making the required modifications.

In conclusion, successful cannabis farming depends on identifying and resolving frequent problems. Growers can prevent or deal with these issues by being informed about typical pests, illnesses, nutrient deficits, and environmental stressors. Maintaining healthy, robust cannabis plants requires early diagnosis, prompt action, and the application of suitable solutions such integrated pest management, disease prevention methods, nutrient supplementation, and environmental control. Growers may overcome typical problems and produce flourishing harvests with large yields and high-quality cannabis by keeping a close eye on issues, taking the right precautions, and acting quickly when necessary.

CHAPTER VI
Harvesting and Curing

Determining the right time to harvest

A vital step in getting the optimal potency, flavor, and general quality of the finished product is harvesting cannabis at the ideal time. Knowing the plant's growth stages, the desired cannabinoid and terpene profiles, and careful observation are all necessary to choose the ideal time to harvest.

Cannabis cultivation depends heavily on timing because the quality and effects of the finished product are directly impacted by harvesting at the right time. While harvesting too late can result in overripe buds with diminished strength and unfavorable flavors, picking too early can result in undeveloped flowers with low THC content. The ideal sensory experience is delivered when the harvest is timed to coincide with the plant's peak cannabinoid and terpene production.

The timing of the harvest is influenced by a number of factors. Given that different strains have distinct growth patterns and maturity times, the particular strain being raised is a crucial factor to take into account. It is essential to comprehend the traits of the strain and its anticipated harvest window in order to choose the right time.

The desired outcomes of the finished product are taken into consideration while choosing the harvest time. Some growers might prefer a more energizing high, indicating an earlier harvest to take advantage of the strain's peak THC content. Others would want a more calming and tranquil high, indicating a somewhat later harvest to promote the growth of cannabinol (CBN). The decision-making process for choosing the harvest window is guided by the desired outcomes.

The intended terpene and cannabinoid characteristics in the finished product can affect when to harvest. During the flowering stage of the plant, different cannabinoids, such as THC and CBD, reach different production peaks. Additionally, terpene profiles can change at this time. Growers may time their harvests to catch the ideal combination of components that give the intended flavor and effects by understanding the target cannabinoid and terpene profiles.

A crucial step in figuring out when to harvest is evaluating the plant's maturity. The plant's readiness can be assessed using a variety of techniques:

Examining the trichomes, the little, resinous structures on the flowers, is one way to do this. Growers can view the trichomes and determine their state of maturity by using a magnifying instrument, such as a jeweler's loupe or a microscope. Trichomes that are clear indicate immaturity, while those that are milky or cloudy indicate the ideal time for harvest. Amber trichomes indicate a later harvest for a distinct cannabinoid profile and point to a more mature stage.

Another visual indicator for determining plant maturity is the color of the pistil. The tiny hairs on flowers called pistils undergo color changes over the course of the flowering cycle. Pistils are typically whitish and lengthy in the early stages. The pistils begin to darken as the plant ages, developing orange or brown tones. The maturity stage of the plant can also be determined by looking at the color of the pistils.

It's also crucial to visually evaluate the flowers' overall look. In general, the presence of fully grown flowers, dense buds, and a thick layer of resin indicates that the crop is ready for harvest. The buds ought to have grown to the ideal size and density, looking strong and healthy.

For the finished product to have the required potency and effects, harvesting during the height of cannabis production is essential. The cannabinoid profiles, notably the concentrations of THC and CBD, are strongly influenced by the time of the harvest. A more elevating impact and lesser THC content may occur from premature harvesting, whereas a more sedative effect and more THC degradation may result from a later harvest. To achieve the intended sensory experience, it is important to strike a balance between the appropriate terpene, cannabinoid, and harvesting characteristics.

Once the best time to harvest has been identified, using the right methods will preserve the product's quality. Timing is key when it comes to harvesting, as doing so when it's cooler outside or when the environmental conditions in the grow room are steady will minimize plant stress and preserve terpene content. By carefully trimming the collected buds, extra leaves and stems are removed, improving the finished product's aesthetic appeal and overall quality. Terpenes, cannabinoids, and tastes must be carefully preserved during the careful drying and curing of the buds. Hanging the buds in a cool, dark, and well-ventilated area while maintaining the proper humidity levels and allowing for gradual moisture loss over time are all essential components of a proper drying and curing process.

In conclusion, determining the appropriate time to harvest is an important stage in growing cannabis because it affects the ultimate product's strength, flavor, and overall quality. Growers can choose the best harvest window by taking into account elements including strain characteristics, desired effects, cannabinoid and terpene profiles, trichome development, and visual cues. The full potential of the grown cannabis is unlocked by harvesting at the peak of cannabinoid production, which guarantees the optimal potency and effects. Growers may produce high-quality, tasty, and strong cannabis harvests that satisfy their desired sensory experiences by using precise timing and appropriate harvesting methods.

Harvesting techniques

Cannabis harvesting is a critical stage in the growing process that has a direct bearing on the end product's quality and yield. The potency, flavors, and overall integrity of the harvested buds must be preserved using proper harvesting methods.

Maintaining the strength and purity of cannabis depends heavily on harvesting practices. Terpenes, cannabinoids, and other significant compounds can be preserved to varying degrees depending on how plants are harvested. Poor harvesting methods can cause deterioration, loss of strength, and flavors that are compromised. Growers may enhance the quality, effects, and overall worth of their harvested buds by using the right approaches.

The choice of when to harvest is influenced by a number of factors:

Determining the ideal harvest time requires evaluating the plant's maturity. In order to determine a plant's maturity, visual indicators including trichome color, pistil development, and bud density are frequently used. Monitoring the plant's growth stage, particularly the flowering phase, also contributes to ensuring that the harvest is ready.

The decision to harvest a crop is heavily influenced by the desired cannabinoid profile. Growers must choose their favorite cannabis combination and harvest in accordance with it because different cannabinoid profiles produce different effects.

Terpenes are in charge of giving cannabis its distinct flavors and fragrances. These sensitive components can be preserved by harvesting at the right time and using the right methods, improving the entire sensory experience of the finished product.

External factors, including temperature, humidity, and light exposure, can affect the decision to harvest. To reduce stress on the plant during harvest, environmental elements must be taken into account.

To determine whether a plant is ready to be harvested, a variety of techniques can be used:

With the aid of a magnifying glass, one can see the trichomes, or small resin glands, on the flowers. The maturity of the plant's cannabinoids is indicated by the color and appearance of the trichomes. Trichomes that are clear or transparent denote immaturity, whereas trichomes that are milky or clouded denote the best time for harvest. Different cannabinoid profiles result from a later harvest, which is indicated by trichomes that are amber or dark.

During the flowering cycle, pistils, the hair-like structures on the flowers, change color. Monitoring the plant's transition from white to orange or brown can reveal information about its maturity.

It is crucial to visually assess how the entire plant and flower appear. Harvest readiness is indicated by fully formed flowers with dense buds, vibrant colors, and abundant resin production.

The following strategies should be taken into account by growers in order to maximize quality and yield during the harvest process:

It is essential to harvest at the ideal time. Pick a period when the environment is stable, as in the colder parts of the day. This lessens stress on the plant and aids in maintaining the potency of terpenes and cannabinoids.

A successful and efficient harvest is ensured by the use of the proper tools and equipment. To avoid contaminating or damaging the product, use disinfected, razor-sharp pruning shears or scissors. To ensure sanitation and hygiene, gloves are advised.

Various harvesting techniques can be used, depending on the size of the plantation. Individual branches or colas can be delicately cut off for small-scale operations using pruning shears or scissors. The entire plant can be severed at the base for larger-scale operations.

Trimming is a crucial step to take after the plant or branches have been harvested to get rid of extra leaves and stems. This enhances the buds' overall quality, potency, and appearance.

The preservation of tastes, smells, and cannabinoids depends on using the right drying and curing methods. Hang the pruned buds in a place that is well-ventilated, cold, dark, and humidified under control. Make sure to keep an eye on the drying process and remove moisture gradually. Following drying, curing in airtight containers enables further taste development and amplification.

It is crucial to store the buds carefully once they have been properly harvested, trimmed, dried, and cured in order to preserve quality over time. The cured and dried buds should be kept out of direct sunlight and excessive moisture in sealed containers. To prevent mold growth, deterioration, or loss of potency, keep the temperature and humidity consistent.

In conclusion, harvesting procedures are an essential part of cannabis production that have a direct bearing on the quality and output of the finished product. Growers can have fruitful and satisfying harvests by being aware of the variables affecting the decision to harvest, using the right procedures for assessing harvest readiness, and putting these approaches into practice to maximize quality and production. The art of timing assures the preservation of cannabinoids, terpenes, tastes, and the general integrity of the collected buds, along with cautious handling, appropriate trimming, and thorough drying and curing procedures. Growers can advance their cannabis cultivation to new heights and provide superior products for the market by mastering harvesting processes.

Drying and curing buds for optimal quality

Bud drying and curing are essential processes in the cannabis cultivation process that have a big impact on the quality, flavor, aroma, and potency of the finished product. These procedures entail the meticulous removal of moisture and the controlled environmental development of desirable characteristics over time. The breakdown of chlorophyll, the decrease of pungent odors, the preservation of cannabinoids and terpenes, the production of complex flavors, and a comfortable smoking experience are all made possible by using the right drying and curing processes.

The quality of cannabis buds must be preserved and improved through drying and curing. These procedures are essential for removing excess moisture, lowering chlorophyll content, enhancing flavor and aroma, and maintaining the potency of terpenes and cannabinoids. The quality and integrity of the buds are long-term preserved by using proper drying and curing processes, which help inhibit the formation of mold and bacteria.

The drying and curing process is influenced by a number of elements, all of which affect the finished product's overall quality:

It's critical to maintain ideal humidity and temperature levels throughout drying and curing. Low humidity can result in excessive drying and harsh flavors, while high humidity might encourage the growth of mold and impair the quality of the buds. 45 to 55 percent relative humidity is good for drying, and 50 to 60 percent for curing. To prevent overly drying out or terpene and cannabinoid degradation, the temperature should be kept between 60 and 70 degrees Fahrenheit (15 and 21 degrees Celsius).

To ensure consistent drying and prevent the growth of mold or mildew, there must be enough ventilation. When the buds are properly ventilated, moisture is continuously eliminated from all of their surfaces, resulting in a more even drying process.

Terpenes and cannabinoids can lose their potency and flavor due to light degradation. To protect the buds from light exposure, it is essential to keep the drying and curing environment dark or to employ UV-blocking materials.

The drying and curing procedure might be affected by whether you decide to dry trimmed buds or whole plants. Drying clipped buds typically results in a more uniform drying process and more effective moisture removal. On the other hand, drying whole plants may help the buds retain more moisture, thereby delaying drying and extending the curing period.

In order to produce the best results and maintain the quality of the buds, proper drying processes are essential:

Trimmed buds are typically dried by being hung upside down on ropes or drying racks. Because of the optimum airflow around the buds, moisture may be removed gradually. Having the buds hung separately or in small groups lessens the chance of mold growth by preventing bud-to-bud contact.

Bud drying can be done quickly and easily with drying racks or nets. To ensure optimal airflow from all sides, the buds are put on racks or nets. Because it maximizes the drying surface, this method might be very helpful for growers with limited space.

Some farmers choose using customized drying chambers or crates with temperature and humidity controls. These systems provide more exact control over the drying procedure, guaranteeing constant airflow and the ideal drying environment.

The gradual process of curing enables the buds' flavor, aroma, and general quality to gradually develop and improve:

Use airtight containers, such as glass jars or food-safe plastic containers, to store dried buds. To ensure appropriate air circulation, fill the containers to roughly 75% of their maximum capacity. During the initial stages of curing, open the containers every day for a short period of time to let out extra moisture. The containers can be opened less frequently as the curing process advances.

Burping includes opening the containers to refill oxygen and expel accumulated moisture. This procedure promotes greater moisture evaporation while assisting in the prevention of mold formation. The frequency of burping steadily diminishes as the buds get to the right level of wetness.

Boveda packs, often referred to as humidity packs, are utilized in the curing containers by some growers. By absorbing or releasing moisture as necessary, these packs help maintain constant humidity levels, creating a steady curing environment.

Long-term curing can be used if you want a flavor and aroma profile that is even more refined. This entails extending the curing process over a number of weeks or even months, enabling the buds to keep acquiring the desired traits. The moisture content of the buds is closely watched during long-term curing, and any indications of mold or deterioration are dealt with right once.

To achieve the greatest results when preserving cannabis, patience and attention to detail are required:

The drying and curing process must be regularly monitored. Regularly assess the moisture level, appearance, and aroma of the buds to make sure they are developing as intended. Measure the humidity levels within the curing containers with hygrometers to gain important insights into the curing process.

A high-quality finished product is only possible with the gradual elimination of moisture. Rushing the drying process can produce excessively dry and harsh buds, while holding onto moisture too long can result in the growth of mold. A progressive and controlled process of moisture removal is ensured by careful observation and adjustment of environmental factors.

It is essential to continuously assess the buds' quality throughout the drying and curing process. To avoid contamination and maintain the general quality of the harvest, remove any buds that exhibit mold or mildew symptoms as once.

It takes time and practice to perfect the skill of drying and curing. Every harvest offers a chance to hone skills and gain a comprehensive understanding of the drying and curing requirements of various strains. Growers can hone their abilities and preferences over time to reliably produce high-quality, palatable, and strong cannabis.

In conclusion, drying and curing buds are important phases in the growth of cannabis that have a significant impact on the quality, flavor, aroma, and potency of the finished product. Growers may protect the quality of their cannabis crop by being patient and precise, recognizing the elements that affect the drying and curing process, and using the right procedures. To maximize the potential of the collected buds, proper moisture removal, progressive curing, and exact environmental control are necessary. Growers can create cannabis of extraordinary quality and provide customers with a genuinely unique cannabis experience by mastering drying and curing procedures.

Storing and preserving harvested cannabis

Cannabis preserving and storage are essential steps in the cultivation process. The potency, flavor, aroma, and overall quality of the collected buds must be preserved using the right preservation methods for a lengthy period of time. Effective storage techniques ensure that the cannabis is kept fresh and potent by protecting the sensitive ingredients such as terpenes and cannabinoids.

For the collected buds to retain their strength and quality, cannabis must be stored and preserved. Cannabis can gradually lose its favorable qualities, such as flavor, aroma, and strength, if it is not stored properly. Cannabinoids, terpenes, and other delicate compounds must be preserved using effective storage methods in order for the cannabis to stay fresh and potent for a lengthy period of time.

The cannabis storage conditions is influenced by a number of factors:

Terpenes and cannabinoids are both significantly degraded by light. These substances may degrade when exposed to UV radiation, losing their efficacy and flavor. Avoiding direct sunlight while storing cannabis in a dark setting helps maintain its quality.

Cannabis needs a certain temperature to stay fresh and last a long time. The degradation process can be accelerated by too much heat, which will result in the loss of potency and terpene profiles. To slow down the degradation process, cannabis should ideally be stored in a cold atmosphere, particularly below 70°F (21°C).

For the texture of the buds to be preserved and mold from growing, the right humidity levels are essential. While extremely dry circumstances can make the buds brittle and harsh, an excess of moisture can result in mold and mildew. For cannabis storage, the optimal relative humidity (RH) is from 59% to 63%.

In order to minimize the buildup of moisture and stagnant air, which can facilitate the growth of mold, proper airflow is required. By allowing for air exchange, adequate ventilation lowers the possibility of humidity-related problems.

Cannabinoids and terpenes can oxidize and degrade more quickly when exposed to too much oxygen. While some contact to oxygen is important for proper curing, limiting prolonged exposure can help keep cannabis fresh and potent.

Growers can use the following procedures to ensure the best possible preservation of their harvested cannabis:

Glass jars with airtight sealing are a common and reliable way to store cannabis. Glass jars offer a stable and controlled environment that shields the buds from the elements while only allowing a small amount of oxygen to reach them. The amount of cannabis being stored should be accommodated by the size of the jars, with little room for air inside.

To store the glass jars, find a room that is cool and dark, such as a pantry or a special cabinet. Avoid regions with changing temperatures, direct sunlight, or areas close to heat sources. The integrity of the buds is preserved when temperature and humidity are stable.

Desiccant packs can be added to storage containers to help absorb extra moisture and maintain the right amounts of humidity. For this, desiccant packs containing silica gel are frequently employed. Place one or two packs into the storage container, making sure they don't touch the marijuana.

Long-term storage can be accomplished using vacuum-sealed bags. Excess oxygen is removed during vacuum sealing, lowering the possibility of oxidation and deterioration. However, take care not to overly squeeze the buds as this can harm their structure.

If it's required to keep big amounts of cannabis for a long time, refrigeration or freezing may be a good alternative for long-term storage. However, it's crucial to keep in mind that changes in temperature and humidity after removing the cannabis from the freezer or refrigerator might have an effect on the quality of the buds. It's best to employ freezing as a last resort because it can also result in textural alterations and even degraded trichomes.

It is essential to maintain stable environmental conditions in order to preserve cannabis:

Check the storage conditions frequently to make sure the temperature and humidity levels stay within the required range. Use thermometers to precisely track temperature and hygrometers to detect humidity.

Keep the cannabis in dark, opaque containers, or use UV-blocking glass jars to keep it away from light. This keeps the potency and terpene profiles intact while reducing exposure to dangerous UV radiation.

Make sure the storage area has adequate ventilation and airflow to avoid the buildup of stale air and extra moisture. Cannabis should not be kept in moist or moldy environments like basements or other enclosed spaces.

Check the cannabis that has been stored frequently for evidence of mold, mildew, or deterioration. To avoid infection, throw away any contaminated buds.

While using the right storage methods, cannabis can be kept for longer periods of time, it will eventually deteriorate over time. Take into account the following to increase the shelf life:

Before storing, make sure the collected cannabis has been thoroughly dried and cured. Inadequately dried buds may retain too much moisture, which can cause mold to grow and the buds to degrade while being stored.

Divide bigger cannabis amounts into more compact, tightly-sealed containers. While the remainder of the stockpile is kept sealed and safe, this enables you to access and use lesser quantities.

If you're storing cannabis in various batches, think about using the oldest stock first. The risk of degradation is reduced by this rotation strategy, which helps ensure that no batch sits idle for an extended amount of time.

In conclusion, it is essential to store and preserve harvested cannabis in order to preserve its quality, strength, flavor, and aroma throughout time. Growers can successfully maintain the integrity of the buds by managing environmental elements such light exposure, temperature, humidity, ventilation, and oxygen exposure. The best preservation is possible with the use of appropriate storage techniques, such as the use of glass jars, desiccant packs, vacuum-sealed bags, cautious refrigeration or freezing. Cannabis that has been stored is regularly inspected and monitored to assist quickly find any problems. Growers that understand the art of storage may guarantee that their cannabis will keep its potency, freshness, and pleasurable qualities, giving users a constant and rewarding cannabis experience.

CHAPTER
VII
Troubleshooting
and Common Issues

Pests and diseases

The health and total productivity of cannabis plants can be greatly impacted by a variety of pests and illnesses. Understanding common pests and diseases and putting them into practice are vital for cannabis growers to have a successful journey through cultivation.

Common Cannabis Pests:

Spider mites are microscopic arachnids that feed on plant sap, which causes stippling, webbing, and yellowing of the leaves. Infestations of spider mites can be controlled by doing routine inspections, maintaining ideal humidity levels, and introducing helpful predators like ladybugs.

Small insects called aphids suck on plant sap, which leads to abnormal growth and the spread of viruses. To reduce aphid numbers, parasitic wasps and lacewings, two natural predators, can be introduced. A spray made of water and mild soap can also keep aphids away.

Thrips are tiny insects that harm buds and cause silver-gray discoloration by feeding on foliage and flowers. Thrips infestations can be controlled by regular observation, maintenance of clean growing environments, and the use of sticky traps.

Whiteflies are tiny, winged insects that feed on plant sap, which causes wilting, yellowing, and the development of sticky honeydew on the leaves. Whitefly numbers can be managed by using yellow sticky traps and importing natural predators like Encarsia wasps.

Small flying insects known as fungus gnats prefer damp soil and eat organic substances. They can spread illnesses and harm roots. To control fungus gnat populations, let the soil dry out between waterings and use sticky traps.

Common Cannabis Diseases:

A fungal disease called powdery mildew causes white, powdery growths on leaves, stems, and buds. Powdery mildew can be prevented and controlled with the help of proper air circulation, maintaining ideal humidity levels, and applying organic fungicides.

A fungus called botrytis causes bud rot, which results in the formation of gray mold on flowers. Botrytis can be avoided and managed with the use of adequate airflow, optimal humidity levels, removing afflicted buds, and the use of fungicides.

Cannabis plants frequently get infected by the fungus gray mold, especially during times of excessive humidity. Gray mold can be prevented from growing and spreading by performing routine pruning, ensuring good air circulation, and lowering humidity levels.

Different fungal infections, which are brought on by overwatering or poorly drained soil, induce root rot. Root rot can be avoided by utilizing helpful bacteria, making sure that proper watering procedures are followed, and ensuring adequate drainage.

The vascular system of cannabis plants is harmed by the soil-borne fungal disease known as fusarium wilt, which results in wilting, stunted growth, and yellowing leaves. Fusarium wilt can be avoided by using strains that are disease-resistant, using crop rotation, and maintaining good soil.

Keeping growth areas clean and sanitary can aid in preventing the spread of pests and illnesses. Keep tools, equipment, and growing spaces regularly clean to reduce the risk of contamination.

Using a combination of preventive measures, cultural practices, and biological controls to manage pests and illnesses is known as integrated pest management (IPM). This strategy comprises ongoing observation, the introduction of advantageous predators, crop rotation, and the use of organic pest management techniques.

The risk of fungal infections is decreased by ensuring sufficient air circulation and ventilation within the grow area. This helps minimize the building of dampness. Use fans and exhaust systems to keep the airflow at its best.

Before adding fresh plants or clones to the main grow area, quarantining them enables examination and detection of any potential pests or illnesses. This prevents infection from spreading throughout the entire crop.

Neem oil, insecticidal soaps, and natural predators are a few examples of organic pest control strategies that can effectively manage pest populations while using fewer harmful chemicals.

The risk of infestations and illnesses can be greatly decreased by choosing cannabis strains that are renowned for their resistance to widespread pathogens and pests. Choose strains based on research that have qualities that are appropriate for your particular growing environment.

For effective management of diseases and pests, early detection is essential. Examine plants frequently for symptoms of illnesses or pests, such as unusual coloring, wilting, deformed growth, or the presence of bugs. If a problem is found, act right away by eliminating the infected plant material, using the proper remedies (chemical or organic), and modifying the environment to stop the problem from spreading.

In conclusion, protecting cannabis plants from pests and diseases calls for an integrated and proactive strategy. Growers can protect their crops and guarantee a healthy and fruitful harvest by becoming aware with common pests and diseases, taking preventive measures, and using effective management techniques. A flourishing cannabis garden requires regular monitoring, maintaining good hygiene, encouraging airflow, and using organic pest control techniques. Growers who are diligent and knowledgeable can maximize output potential, reduce the effects of pests and illnesses, and enjoy the results of their labors.

Nutrient deficiencies and excesses

The production of cannabis plants requires proper nutrient management. Plant health, development, and output can all be significantly impacted by nutrient excesses and deficits. Understanding the signs, causes, and treatments of nutritional imbalances is crucial for cannabis growers in order to give their plants the best nutrition possible for healthy and robust growth.

To grow to their maximum capacity, cannabis plants require a balanced diet. Micronutrients (iron, magnesium, zinc, etc.) and macronutrients (nitrogen, phosphorus, potassium) play important roles in a variety of physiological activities, including photosynthesis, root development, and total plant growth. Nutrient imbalances may impede these procedures and have a negative impact on the health, productivity, and cannabis production of plants.

Common Nutrient Deficiencies:

A lack of nitrogen causes older leaves to turn yellow, limited development, and decreased vigor. It interferes with plant growth and lowers total yield. Nitrogen deficits can be resolved by adding organic matter or fertilizer that is rich in nitrogen.

Lack of phosphorus causes leaves to turn purple or darken, stunts the growth of buds, and delays flowering. Plant growth and reproduction are adversely impacted. Phosphorus deficits can be treated by using organic amendments or fertilizers high in phosphorus.

Lack of potassium results in weakening stems, diminished vigor, and yellowing and necrosis of the leaf edges. It has a detrimental effect on a plant's overall health, resilience, and structure. Deficiencies can be treated by using potassium-rich fertilizers or potassium sulfate.

Young leaves yellow when iron levels are low, but the veins stay green. It reduces photosynthesis and has an impact on chlorophyll synthesis. Iron shortages can be treated by employing iron chelates or iron-rich amendments.

Magnesium shortage results in interveinal yellowing, which gives leaves a marbling appearance. Overall plant development and chlorophyll synthesis are impaired. Magnesium deficiency can be treated with foliar sprays or by rubbing magnesium sulfate on the surface.

Common Nutrient Excesses:

The development of buds and flowers can be sacrificed in favor of lush, dark green foliage when nitrogen levels are too high. At the expense of reproductive growth, it encourages vegetative growth. Nitrogen surpluses can be resolved by changing fertilizer ratios or lowering nitrogen inputs.

Excessive phosphorus can impede the intake of nutrients, which can result in deficits of other elements. Additionally, it may lead to soil imbalances and nutrient lockout. To avoid phosphorus excesses, proper soil testing and fertilization procedures must be adjusted.

Inadequate potassium levels can affect how nutrients are absorbed and cause calcium and magnesium levels to be out of balance. Additionally, it may obstruct the intake of water and cause nutrient shortages. To prevent excesses, potassium levels must be maintained through proper fertilization methods and soil testing.

Excessive calcium can prevent the body from absorbing other vital nutrients, especially magnesium and potassium. Nutrient imbalances and effects on plant development and health may emerge from it. It's crucial to maintain the proper calcium levels in the soil through balanced fertilizer.

Unbalances can result from pH levels that are too high or too low, which might impact the availability of nutrients. The intake and usage of vital nutrients can be impacted by altered pH levels, which can have an impact on a plant's overall health. It's critical to maintain the proper pH range for cannabis cultivation to avoid nutritional imbalances.

Strategies for Achieving Balanced Nutrition:

Regular soil testing identifies nutrient excesses or deficits, enabling focused modifications to fertilization techniques. Informed nutrient management decisions are made possible by the useful information that soil testing offer about the nutrient state of the soil.

Use nutrition blends or balanced fertilizers created especially for growing cannabis. For the best plant growth, these formulas offer a wide variety of important macronutrients and micronutrients.

Compost, worm castings, or well-rotted manure are examples of organic amendments that feed the soil with slow-release nutrients, enhancing soil structure and nutrient availability. Nutrient management can be done sustainably with the use of organic additives.

Controlled-release fertilizers reduce the possibility of nutrient imbalances by supplying nutrients gradually and continuously over an extended period of time. These fertilizers make sure that nutrients are consistently available, promoting strong plant development.

By spraying a nutritional solution directly onto the leaves, foliar feeding enables quick nutrient absorption. When prompt action is required, this technique can aid in addressing nutrient deficiencies quickly.

To keep the pH of the soil or growing medium within the appropriate range for cannabis cultivation, regularly check it and make adjustments. Maintaining proper pH levels is essential for ensuring balanced nutrition since pH levels affect the availability and uptake of nutrients.

In conclusion, balanced nutrition is essential for the wellbeing, development, and productivity of cannabis plants. It is crucial to comprehend the signs, causes, and treatments of nutrient excesses and shortages in order to produce the best cultivation outcomes. An active strategy for nutrient management is made possible by consistent soil testing, appropriate fertilization, and the use of organic amendments. Growers can maximize yield potential, encourage the production of high-quality cannabinoid-rich harvests, and ensure healthy, vigorous growth by providing cannabis plants with the ideal ratio of macronutrients and micronutrients.

Environmental factors affecting plant health

For cannabis plants to grow and thrive, ideal environmental conditions must be created and maintained. Light, temperature, humidity, airflow, and carbon dioxide (CO_2) levels, among other environmental elements, have a substantial impact on plant growth, metabolism, and general productivity. Understanding how these elements interact and impact plant health is crucial for cannabis growers to achieve effective production.

Cannabis plant health and growth are greatly influenced by light, a crucial environmental factor:

For photosynthesis and various growth phases, cannabis plants need certain light wavelengths. Red light (600–700 nm) is necessary for flowering, while blue light (400–500 nm) encourages vegetative growth. Plant growth is optimized when the proper light spectrum is provided, either by utilizing full-spectrum grow lights or by altering the light cycle.

The rate of photosynthesis and plant development are both directly impacted by light intensity. Stretched, feeble growth is the result of insufficient light, while light burn and nutrient imbalances are the results of too much light. Maintaining the ideal light intensity involves adjusting the distance between the light source and the plants.

various growth stages of cannabis plants require various amounts of light. Maximizing the potential for production and inducing flowering depend on maintaining regular light/dark cycles. Plant growth and development are regulated by varying the length of exposure to light during the vegetative and flowering phases.

The metabolism, enzymatic activity, and general health of plants are all significantly influenced by temperature:

Cannabis plants require a certain range of temperatures to thrive. Normal growth conditions are typically thought to be daytime temperatures of 70–85°F (21–29°C) and nighttime temperatures of 60–70°F (15–21°C). Outside of this range, temperatures can have a negative effect on the health and productivity of plants.

Heat stress, which can result in wilting, leaf curling, and decreased growth, can be brought on by temperatures that are over the ideal range. Utilizing cooling strategies like ventilation, fans, or air conditioning assists in controlling temperature and preventing heat exhaustion.

Low temperatures outside of the ideal range can cause cold stress, which slows growth, depletes nutrients, and makes a plant more vulnerable to disease. During colder months, maintaining the right temperatures is made easier by using heating equipment or insulating the growth area.

Transpiration, nutritional uptake, and illness risk are all influenced by humidity levels:

Cannabis plants demand greater humidity levels during the vegetative period, which ranges from 40-70%. This range encourages healthy root development, foliar growth, and transpiration.

To reduce the risk of mold and bud rot, lower humidity levels of about 40–50% are advised during the flowering stage. Humidity levels can be managed with the use of effective air circulation and dehumidification methods like exhaust fans or dehumidifiers.

Overly humid conditions can cause condensation on leaves, which encourages the growth of diseases. Condensation-related problems can be reduced by maintaining proper humidity levels, improving air circulation, and avoiding overwatering.

Proper ventilation and air circulation are essential for preserving plant health.

A sufficient airflow allows for the exchange of CO_2, which is crucial for photosynthesis. CO_2 levels that are enough promote plant growth and production. Optimizing CO_2 availability involves having good airflow and, if necessary, adopting CO_2 supplementation methods.

High humidity, poor gas exchange, and the buildup of microorganisms are all consequences of stagnant air. The risk of sickness is decreased by using oscillating fans, exhaust fans, and venting devices to guarantee optimum air circulation.

CO_2 concentrations affect plant production and growth:

CO_2 levels between 1000 and 1500 parts per million (ppm) are ideal for cannabis plants to grow during the day. This concentration encourages photosynthesis, which results in faster growth and greater harvests.

Utilizing CO2 generators or tanks to enhance CO2 levels in enclosed or indoor areas can promote plant development and increase yield potential. To avoid too much or too little CO2, it is crucial to monitor and regulate CO2 levels based on the individual growth stage.

In conclusion, environmental conditions have a big impact on the growth and health of cannabis plants. Growers can produce the best growth conditions for their cannabis crop by understanding the impacts of light, temperature, humidity, air movement, and CO2 levels. Healthy plant growth, higher yields, and high-quality harvests are facilitated by providing the right light spectrum, maintaining the right temperature and humidity ranges, guaranteeing adequate air circulation, and optimizing CO2 levels. Growers may maintain robust, resilient cannabis plants and achieve good cultivation outcomes by skillfully regulating these environmental parameters.

CHAPTER VIII
Advanced Techniques

Hydroponic cultivation

Cannabis farmers are increasingly turning to the soilless technique of hydroponic cultivation since it allows more finer control over fertilizer supply, faster growth rates, and greater yields. This technique substitutes a water-based nutritional solution for traditional soil by allowing plants to flourish. A fertilizer solution specifically formulated to meet the demands of cannabis plants, a substrate or medium to support root structure and retain moisture, and pH and electrical conductivity (EC) regulation to assure nutrient availability are the guiding principles of hydroponics.

The advantages of hydroponic cultivation are numerous. First, it improves nutrient uptake, making it possible for cannabis plants to take in nutrients more effectively, leading to faster growth rates. Second, hydroponics contributes to water conservation because recirculating systems use less water than conventional soil-based farming methods. This controlled setting enables effective water management, lowering waste and adverse environmental effects. The ability to precisely manage environmental elements like temperature, light exposure, pH levels, and nutrient content is another benefit of hydroponics. With the help of this control, farmers can enhance the growing environment, encouraging the growth of healthier, more robust plants. Furthermore, compared to conventional soil-based approaches, cannabis plants cultivated hydroponically develop vegetatively more quickly, flower earlier, and produce higher yields. The lack of soil eliminates the possibility of soil-borne pathogens, and the regulated environment reduces the entry of pests, hence hydroponic systems offer lower risks of soil-borne diseases and pests.

There are numerous hydroponic systems available for growing cannabis. A continuous flow of nutrient solution is applied to the roots using the Nutrient Film Technique (NFT). Through bubbling air stones, Deep Water Culture (DWC) suspends the roots in a nutrient-rich solution and continuously supplies them with nutrients and oxygen. Ebb and Flow systems ensure oxygenation and efficient nutrient delivery by periodically flooding the growing medium with the nutrient solution and then draining it back into a reservoir. By suspending the roots in the air and spraying them with nutritional solution on a regular basis, aeroponics maximizes oxygenation and nutrient absorption. Growers should make their decision based on their unique needs and available resources because each system has advantages.

Success in hydroponic agriculture depends on addressing a number of crucial issues. Optimal nutrient absorption and the prevention of imbalances are ensured by routine testing and adjusting of the composition and concentration of the nutrient solution. The health and vitality of cannabis plants are dependent on high-quality, contaminant-free water that is also the right temperature and pH balance. The correct grow lights must be chosen, and LEDs offer energy-efficient, tunable illumination spectrums adapted to the particular requirements of cannabis plants. Controlling temperature and humidity is also crucial since healthy plant growth is aided by certain temperature ranges and humidity levels. In hydroponic systems, it's crucial to keep an eye on the condition of the roots since routine checks prevent infections, algae growth, and root rot from spreading. Root health is supported by enough oxygenation, suitable water levels, and avoiding overwatering.

While hydroponic cultivation has many advantages, there are also some possible drawbacks. If nutrient levels are not consistently monitored and changed, nutrient imbalances may develop, resulting in toxicities or deficiencies. Cleaning equipment, keeping an eye on pH and EC levels, and avoiding clogging or obstructions in irrigation systems are all important aspects of proper maintenance. Successful hydroponic growing relies heavily on technical expertise and experience. To maximize plant growth, growers must become knowledgeable about nutrient management, system setup, and troubleshooting methods.

In conclusion, soilless hydroponic growing enhances nutrient uptake, quickens growth rates, and boosts overall yields for cannabis growers. Growers may produce the best possible growing conditions for cannabis plants by comprehending the basics of hydroponics, choosing the right systems, and putting effective fertilizer management, temperature control, and lighting methods into practice. Hydroponic cannabis growing is a desirable choice for both small-scale and commercial cannabis production because of the advantages of water conservation, precise environmental control, disease avoidance, and rapid growth. Hydroponic growers can realize the full potential of cannabis growing, reaching remarkable plant health and maximizing the quality and quantity of their harvests, with careful attention to detail and ongoing learning.

Sea of Green (SOG) method

Cannabis farmers frequently employ the Sea of Green (SOG) approach to boost yields and optimize space use. The SOG method's main idea is to grow many of little plants close together so they can rapidly and effectively fill the space. With the help of early flowering induction, low vegetative growth, and a high plant density strategy, growers may produce large and quick harvests.

Increased yield is one of the SOG method's key advantages. Growers are able to more efficiently use the available space and increase their output per square foot by cultivating a number of tiny plants near together. This is especially helpful for growers that have limited space or want to increase their crops. In comparison to other training methods, the SOG method provides a shorter growing cycle. Growers can harvest their crops earlier and possibly have many harvests in a single season by causing early flowering.

Increased light penetration is a benefit of the SOG approach. When there are many little plants, light can reach more bud locations and encourage better bud growth all over the plant. As a result, the quality and potency are improved overall. Additionally, the SOG method's reduced vegetative growth promotes greater air circulation and flow within the canopy. This encourages healthier plants and helps minimize the buildup of humidity, which lowers the chance of mold or mildew.

Growers need take into account a few crucial strategies in order to successfully use the SOG approach. The choice of plants is important since selecting cannabis strains that work well with the SOG approach can improve outcomes significantly. Look for strains with traits such as many, compact colas and quick flowering. Techniques for pruning and training are also crucial in the SOG approach. The plant's energy can be redirected to the higher canopy by pruning lower branches and leaves and using procedures like topping or FIMing, which encourage bushier growth and more colas.

To provide even light distribution across the canopy using the SOG approach, lighting optimization is essential. To maximize light penetration, this can entail using several light sources or utilizing reflective surfaces. Another crucial factor to take into account is nutrient management, since the shorter vegetative phase might necessitate alterations to nutrient levels and feeding schedules. The amount of nutrients should be regularly checked and adjusted in order to ensure optimal plant health and avoid hazardous or deficient nutrition conditions.

The SOG approach has several advantages, but there are some possible drawbacks as well. It is crucial to make sure each plant has enough light, nutrients, and water because growing many little plants in a small area might create competition for resources. The high plant density of the SOG approach can make it more difficult to handle diseases and pests. It is essential to implement strict hygiene procedures, regular inspections, and preventative measures including integrated pest management (IPM) techniques.

In conclusion, the Sea of Green (SOG) approach is a very efficient way for maximizing cannabis yields and making effective use of available space. Growers can obtain amazing yields and speedy harvests by employing high plant density, promoting early flowering, and minimizing vegetative growth. Shorter growing cycles, higher light penetration, and effective space usage are just a few advantages of the SOG approach. Growers may unlock the full potential of the SOG approach and advance their cannabis cultivation to new heights with careful plant selection, pruning, training, lighting optimization, and nutrient management.

Screen of Green (SCROG) method

Cannabis growers who want to increase their yields and produce an even canopy of buds frequently use the Screen of Green (SCROG) technique. The SCROG method has a number of advantages since it trains plants and encourages lateral development by using a screen or mesh.

A plant training approach called Screen of Green (SCROG) focuses on developing a uniform, horizontal canopy of cannabis plants. With the help of a screen or mesh suspended above the plants, the branches are trained to develop horizontally, improving light distribution and promoting bud development. The SCROG method's guiding principles include the effective management of plant development, the positioning of screens, and plant training.

The possibility for higher yields is the main benefit of using the SCROG method in cannabis production. Growers can make an even canopy with more bud sites by training the plants to grow horizontally and spreading out the branches. This results in more colas and an overall higher yield per square foot. Additionally, the SCROG approach encourages better light distribution, making certain that each bud receives the right amount of light. This results in more consistent bud development and improved bud quality overall.

The SCROG method can be used for both indoor and outdoor cultivation because it efficiently utilizes space. Growers can maximize their growth area and utilize their limited space by teaching the plants to grow horizontally. This is especially helpful for growers who have small grow spaces or who want to maximize their output potential in a short space.

The SCROG approach must be applied with meticulous attention to detail and strict adherence to predetermined procedures. The first step in the process is to choose a screen or mesh that is suitable, durable enough to sustain the weight of the plants, and with spaces that are the right size for weaving the branches through. Since gardeners should start training the plants when they are in the vegetative stage and have enough branches to weave through the screen, timing is crucial. The SCROG procedure must include topping and pruning the plants to regulate vertical development and encourage lateral branching.

Growers delicately thread the branches through the screen's openings as the plants grow to direct their growth horizontally. To keep the canopy at an even height, the branches must be adjusted and secured on a regular basis. The SCROG technique also depends heavily on effective light management. To guarantee even light distribution across the canopy, growers must move the grow lights into the proper position. To reach the lower bud sites, it might be necessary to modify the lamps' height or angle. Techniques like leaf tucking and pruning can be used to increase ventilation and light penetration within the canopy.

The SCROG approach has several advantages, but there are also possible drawbacks. The training procedure takes time and work because the branches need to be monitored and adjusted on a regular basis as the canopy grows. Maintenance is also essential to avoid the accumulation of humidity, mold, or pests inside the dense canopy. As not all cannabis strains react to the SCROG procedure similarly, strain compatibility is another aspect to take into account. Successful SCROG cultivation depends on the careful selection of strains with good lateral branching and mild stretch during the flowering stage.

The Screen of Green (SCROG) approach is a useful strategy for enhancing cannabis canopies and raising yields, in conclusion. The plants can be trained to grow horizontally through a screen or mesh, which allows growers to distribute high-quality buds evenly. Increased yields, better light distribution, effective space utilization, and greater bud quality are just a few benefits of the SCROG method. However, it necessitates meticulous attention to detail, intelligent strain selection, and consistent maintenance. Cannabis producers can generate astounding yields and improve the quality of their harvests by properly implementing the SCROG method.

Breeding and genetics

Fundamental elements of cannabis growing that have transformed the industry are breeding and genetics. Cannabis growers have unlocked a wide variety of strains with a variety of characteristics and capabilities through selective breeding and careful genetic manipulation.

Cannabis plants are intentionally chosen and crossed in the breeding process to create offspring with desired characteristics. The genetic diversity found in cannabis populations serves as the foundation for breeding theory. Every cannabis plant has a distinct collection of genes that control its physical and chemical characteristics. Breeders can produce new strains with the required qualities by selecting breeding plants with those traits.

The core principle of cannabis genetic development is selective breeding. Plants with desirable characteristics like yield, potency, aroma, flavor, or disease resistance are carefully selected by breeders, who then cross them to create offspring with a combination of these characteristics. The intended features grow increasingly prominent and persistent through subsequent breeding generations, resulting in the development of distinctive and specialized strains.

Cannabis breeders use a variety of methods to influence the genetics and accomplish their breeding goals. Typical strategies include:

Plant phenotypes, such as plant structure, leaf shape, flower morphology, scent, and resin production, are used by breeders to assess plants. For further breeding, plants with desirable characteristics are chosen.

In order to merge the qualities of two individual cannabis plants, which each have distinct characteristics, they must be crossed. Breeders can introduce novel genetic fusions using this method, promoting diversity and broadening the selection of breeds.

Crossing closely related plants, such as siblings or parent-offspring crosses, is referred to as inbreeding. By encouraging genetic consistency within a strain, this method aids in stabilizing and reinforcing good features.

When two genetically diverse strains are crossed, the result is a hybridization that combines characteristics from both parent plants. This method has produced a large number of hybrid strains, each with their own distinctive traits.

Based on desirable qualities, breeders carefully choose specific plants from a population to reproduce through cloning or seed production. The perpetuation of good genetic features is ensured by this strategy.

Both commercial and recreational cannabis growers are affected by breeding and genetics. Breeding enables commercial producers to create strains that are suited to customer desires and market trends. To design strains that target particular market niches, breeders concentrate on characteristics like high yield, disease resistance, terpene profiles, or THC content. This makes it possible for producers to produce cannabis that satisfies the various demands and tastes of consumers.

In the medical cannabis sector, breeding also has a big impact. Breeders can produce strains that are well-suited for therapeutic uses by selecting breeding plants with particular cannabinoid profiles, such as high CBD or THC concentration. This makes it easier to create cannabis-based treatments for particular illnesses and disorders, giving patients more specialized treatment alternatives.

Breeding offers a way for cannabis enthusiasts and home growers to experiment and customize. By experimenting with various genetic combinations, enthusiasts can develop distinctive cultivars that represent their individual preferences. Breeding additionally enables the perpetuation of heirloom or rare strains that could otherwise disappear over time, maintaining their accessibility for subsequent generations.

It is critical to think about moral and responsible breeding practices as breeding methods progress. Breeders should put genetic diversity first and steer clear of relying too much on a small number of well-liked breeds. The possibility for future breeding improvements is increased by maintaining a large genetic pool, which also encourages long-term sustainability and genetic resilience.

Responsible breeding requires complete disclosure of genetic lineages and proper documentation of those lineages. Breeders may then accurately describe the genetic composition and characteristics of their breeds, enabling customers to make knowledgeable decisions. Within the breeding community, transparency and cooperation encourage cooperation, innovation, and knowledge exchange.

In conclusion, breeding and genetics are the foundation of cannabis cultivation and allow producers to fully utilize the plant's potential. Breeders can produce cannabis strains with a variety of desired characteristics by using selective breeding. The knowledge and practices of breeding enable the creation of specific strains suited for industrial and medical uses. Furthermore, breeding enables cannabis enthusiasts to experiment with and develop their own distinctive varieties. Breeders must prioritize genetic diversity, maintain moral breeding standards, and advance industry transparency. Cultivators may unleash the full potential of cannabis and contribute to the continued evolution of this unique plant by knowing the concepts and methods of breeding.

CHAPTER
IX
Responsible
and Ethical Cultivation

Safety precautions

Cannabis growing places a high priority on safety measures to protect the health and welfare of producers, employees, and customers. Prioritizing safety measures is crucial to reduce hazards and maintain a secure workplace as the cannabis business expands.

Cannabis cultivation calls for the careful observance of safety precautions to guard against potential dangers. To protect the wellbeing and safety of those participating in cultivation, the following actions should be taken:

For workers to be protected from potential risks during cannabis growing, personal protective equipment is crucial. Gloves, safety glasses, respirators, and coveralls are examples of PPE. These products reduce the possibility of chemical exposure, bodily harm, and other potential risks. Workers can greatly lower their risk of accidents and injuries by putting on the proper PPE.

In the cultivation of cannabis, chemicals like pesticides, fertilizers, and cleaning products are frequently employed. It is essential to handle and store these chemicals properly to protect worker safety and avoid environmental pollution. It is important to carefully read and comprehend the manufacturer's instructions, which cover dosage, application techniques, and safety measures. Additionally, chemicals need to be properly labeled, stored in approved locations, and kept away from consumables like food and cannabis plants. When dealing with chemicals, adequate ventilation should be given to reduce exposure.

In cannabis growth facilities, electrical safety is crucial to prevent accidents, fires, or electrocutions. To ensure adherence to regional building norms and regulations, only licensed electricians should be involved for electrical system installation and maintenance. To reduce electrical dangers, proper wiring, grounding, and routine inspections are essential. Easy access, clear labeling, and an unobstructed view of electrical panels are all requirements. Water and electricity should never be combined, and outlets in locations where water may be present should have waterproof covers.

Facilities used for cannabis growing are prone to fires since they contain electrical machinery, lighting systems, and possibly combustible components. To lessen the likelihood of fires and guarantee the security of those who work in the facility, fire prevention measures should be put into place. This involves placing fire extinguishers in easily accessible areas, using smoke detectors and fire alarms, storing combustible products properly, and keeping emergency exits open and unblocked.

To protect the security of cannabis cultivation, regulatory compliance is essential. To comply with the requirements for licensing, permits, zoning, construction codes, and safety laws, one must be familiar with local, state, and federal regulations. Prioritizing worker safety is crucial, as is offering thorough instruction on safety measures, hazard recognition, and emergency procedures. In accordance with environmental rules, proper waste disposal procedures and recycling programs should be put into place. It is essential to keep precise records of safety procedures followed, chemical consumption, training, inspections, and incident reports in order to show compliance and promote continual improvement.

In conclusion, safety measures are crucial in cannabis growing to safeguard the health and welfare of producers, employees, and customers. Cultivators can make sure that their business is safe and responsible by using personal protective equipment, managing chemicals correctly, electrical safety precautions, fire prevention procedures, and complying with regulatory requirements. Safety is given first priority as this not only safeguards those working in the growing process but also helps the cannabis sector be viable and prosper in the long run. Cultivators can grow cannabis in a way that upholds the highest standards of health and wellbeing by using these safety measures.

Legal considerations and compliance

In the world of cannabis cultivation, compliance with the law and legal issues are of the utmost importance. Cultivators must understand the intricate web of rules as the cannabis sector develops in order to guarantee compliance with the law.

To operate lawfully, cannabis growers must first obtain the proper licenses and permits. Depending on the jurisdiction, different procedures may apply, however fees, background checks, and application processes are usually required. The license procedure must be followed in full by cultivators, who must also present correct and comprehensive documentation, meet the necessary financial and security standards, and abide by any limits or conditions set by the licensing authorities.

Zoning and land use regulations which dictate where agricultural activities can be located apply to cannabis cultivation. Cannabis growing may only be allowed in certain zones or locations, according to local legislation. The distance from schools or other sensitive places, as well as any other land use limitations, must be kept in mind by cultivators while planning their operations. It is essential to comprehend and abide by local zoning laws in order to stay in compliance and prevent legal problems.

Cannabis growers must follow strict product safety and labeling guidelines in order to safeguard consumers and guarantee compliance with legal laws. This covers quality assurance procedures, testing for contaminants, and appropriate cannabis product labeling and packaging. To make sure that the products are safe for consumption, cultivators must adhere to the established requirements for testing, which includes checking for pesticides, heavy metals, and microbiological contaminants. Furthermore, it is crucial that product labels are precise and compliant, offering details like potency, strain name, dosing recommendations, and necessary warnings.

Security measures are an essential component of legal compliance given the nature of the cannabis sector. To avoid theft, diversion, or unauthorized access to the production facility, cultivators must put in place strict security protocols. Video surveillance, access control, alarm systems, and inventory tracking are all examples of security measures. The safety and integrity of the cannabis supply chain are ensured as well as the business and its assets by complying with security requirements.

Cannabis growers are required by law to maintain accurate and complete records. Cultivators are required to keep thorough records of all elements of their business, including sales, inventory, testing outcomes, waste disposal, personnel training, and security procedures. These records are used as proof of compliance and might be checked or audited by the authorities. To maintain compliance with regulatory obligations and ease effective reporting and tracking of critical information, cultivators should develop thorough record-keeping practices, including the use of inventory management systems and document preservation regulations.

At the local, state, and federal levels, cannabis growing is governed by a complicated network of laws. Growers need to be careful in keeping up with the changing regulatory environment and making sure that all applicable laws and regulations are being followed. This can entail keeping up with changes in license requirements, comprehending tax liabilities, and obeying environmental laws. Additionally, growers must be aware of any constraints on sales and distribution, prohibitions on promotion and marketing, and adherence to staff health and safety standards.

In conclusion, the profitability and sustainability of cannabis farming operations depend on legal concerns and compliance. Cultivators can operate legally and support the responsible expansion of the cannabis industry by navigating the regulatory environment, obtaining the required licenses and permits, adhering to zoning and land use restrictions, ensuring product safety and labeling, putting in place strong security measures, and keeping meticulous records. To maintain compliance and adherence to the highest standards of legality and integrity in cannabis growing, it is essential to stay informed about how the legal landscape is changing and to stay current on these developments.

Environmental impact and sustainability

Due to increasing demand for both medical and recreational uses, cannabis cultivation has grown quickly in recent years. However, this growth has sparked concerns about how large-scale agricultural operations would affect the environment. To reduce its environmental impact and assure a greener future, the cannabis sector has responded by embracing the need for sustainable practices.

Cannabis cultivation is known for using a lot of electricity, especially indoor growing. Heating, ventilation, and air conditioning (HVAC) systems and grow lights both have large energy requirements. Cultivators can use a number of ways to cut down on energy use and lessen the environmental effect that results from it:

Electricity consumption can be considerably decreased by switching to energy-efficient lighting, such as LED (light-emitting diode) technology. Compared to conventional lighting alternatives, LEDs use less energy, emit less heat, and have a longer lifespan.

Utilize natural sunlight whenever possible by optimizing greenhouse design or implementing light-diffusing techniques. By reducing the need for artificial lighting, this method lowers energy usage.

Utilizing advanced energy management technologies makes it easier to track and manage energy consumption. Based on real-time data, these systems may automatically modify the lighting and HVAC settings to ensure optimum operation and lower unnecessary energy usage.

Adopting sustainable energy practices, such as using solar or wind power, is an essential first step. Electricity usage can be offset and greenhouse gas emissions can be greatly reduced by installing solar panels or collaborating with regional renewable energy suppliers.

Concerns about water conservation and scarcity are spreading throughout many areas. Large amounts of water are needed for cannabis growing, thus effective water management is crucial. The following tactics can be used by cultivators to reduce water usage:

Adopting water-efficient irrigation techniques, such as drip irrigation or micro-sprinklers, reduces water loss due to evaporation or runoff and provides water directly to plant roots.

Closed-loop irrigation system implementation may significantly reduce total water use by capturing and treating runoff or surplus water for reuse.

Rainwater collection and storage can support irrigation needs and lessen dependency on freshwater sources. During the rainy season, collecting rainwater in reservoirs or tanks ensures a reliable water supply during dry periods.

Choose cannabis varieties that require less water or are more tolerant of drought. Water loss can be reduced even further by using cultivation strategies like mulching, which helps preserve soil moisture.

In cannabis growing, waste management is a crucial component of sustainability. Cultivators can lessen landfill waste and environmental contamination by putting appropriate waste management practices into practice. Important waste management techniques include:

Recycling of organic plant waste is made possible by installing on-site composting facilities. Plant trimmings, leaves, and other organic materials are transformed into nutrient-rich compost by composting, which can then be given to nearby gardeners or utilized in cultivation.

Putting in place thorough recycling systems aids in keeping trash like packaging, plastic containers, and paper out of landfills. Work with nearby recycling facilities to coordinate training for staff on effective garbage sorting and recycling techniques.

It is important to properly dispose of pesticide containers, solvents, and other chemicals used in cultivation. Safe disposal of hazardous waste ensured by adherence to regional rules safeguards the environment and public health.

The environmental impact of cultivation activities can be considerably reduced by minimizing waste formation through effective inventory management, careful planning, and the use of environmentally friendly packing materials.

For the sake of the environment, consumer health, and employee welfare, responsible pesticide use is essential. Using integrated pest management (IPM) techniques encourages sustainable pest management:

Give priority to preventive measures including keeping the area around the cultivation site clean, periodically checking plants for pest or disease symptoms, and following good hygiene procedures.

Reduce the need for chemical pesticides by introducing beneficial insects, predators, or pathogens that naturally reduce pests.

Utilize horticulture strategies including crop rotation, companion planting, and keeping adequate airflow to ward off pests and enhance plant health.

When using pesticides, choose those that are low in toxicity and safe for the environment, and always read and follow the label directions. To reduce hazards and guarantee adherence to safety rules, train employees in proper handling, storing, and application methods.

In conclusion, sustainability and the impact on the environment are important factors in the growing of cannabis. Cultivators can drastically lower their ecological footprint by introducing energy-efficient technologies, water conservation measures, waste reduction and recycling initiatives, and responsible pesticide usage. Sustainable cultivation methods help ensure the cannabis industry's long-term profitability while also preserving the environment. Cultivators may contribute to the creation of a greener future while responsibly and sustainably supplying the increasing demand for cannabis products by embracing these methods.

CONCLUSION

Addressing common concerns and misconceptions

Cannabis production has long been controversial, which has led to widespread concerns and misunderstandings about the practice. It is essential to address these concerns and dispel the myths that impede the development of the cannabis industry as it expands and evolves.

Public Health Concerns:

Impacts on Youth: One major concern is that cannabis growing would make it easier for young people to get and use the drug.

Regulatory systems and responsible cultivation techniques can, however, reduce access by minors. Important preventive measures include strict adherence to legal age restrictions and safe storage of cannabis products.

Secondhand smoking: Exposure to secondhand smoking can be an issue in the cannabis industry. However, effective air filtration, ventilation, and smoking bans can all help to reduce possible dangers.

Occupational Health and Safety: Protecting the wellbeing and safety of those who work in the cannabis sector is essential. Cultivators can build a secure workplace by putting in place the right training, offering personal protective equipment, and following occupational health and safety regulations.

Sustainable environmental practices:

Energy Consumption: Although indoor cultivation can be very energy-intensive, growers are increasingly adopting energy-efficient technologies, such as LED lighting and renewable energy sources, in order to reduce their energy consumption and their carbon emissions.

Water Usage: To reduce water use and encourage sustainable cultivation methods, cultivators should use water-saving techniques such effective irrigation systems, water recycling, and rainwater collection.

Waste Management: Cultivators may lessen their environmental effect and support a more sustainable sector by putting recycling systems into place, composting organic waste, and cutting back on packaging waste.

Use of Pesticides: Using pesticides responsibly assures minimal environmental impact while maintaining crop health. This includes integrated pest management (IPM) techniques, organic farming methods, and adherence to safety laws.

Potential for Addiction and Misuse:

Addiction Potential: Although there are concerns about cannabis addiction, research indicates that it has a relatively low potential for addiction when compared to other drugs. Consumers can make educated judgments and encourage responsible use with the aid of ethical cultivation practices and accurate product labeling.

Medical Use: Cannabis is grown for medical as well as recreational purposes. It is essential in delivering therapeutic advantages to people with a range of medical ailments. The safety and effectiveness of medicinal cannabis products are guaranteed by rigorous quality control procedures, standardized dosing, and regulatory oversight.

Legal Considerations:

Compliance with Legal Frameworks: To assure legality, cannabis growing must abide by all applicable municipal, state, and federal laws. Legal compliance depends on obtaining the required licenses, following zoning and land-use regulations, and maintaining accurate records and reporting.

Regulatory Evolution: As cannabis laws continue to change, growers must keep up with the latest developments and modify their procedures accordingly. To maintain continued compliance, this involves keeping an eye on license requirements, taxation laws, and marketing limits.

Illicit Market Displacement: It's a common misperception that the growth of the illicit market is facilitated by legal cannabis growing. However, strong regulatory frameworks, high standards for quality control, and tax income from the legal market can all contribute to replace illegal activity.

In conclusion, it is essential for developing informed discussions and advancing responsible practices that prevalent concerns and misconceptions about cannabis production are cleared up. We can dispel myths and develop a more nuanced view of cannabis growing by providing accurate information about the effects on public health, environmental sustainability, the possibility for addiction, and legal considerations. To ensure that cannabis growing is carried out in a way that prioritizes public health, environmental sustainability, and adherence to legal frameworks, cultivators, regulators, and society at large all have a duty. We can navigate the complicated world of cannabis cultivation, get its rewards to the fullest, and reduce any potential risks by being informed and having open discussions.

Final tips and encouragement for novice growers

It can be thrilling and difficult for a novice grower to begin the path of cannabis cultivation. It's crucial to arm yourself with knowledge, planning, and the proper mindset as you enter into the realm of plant care.

Planning and research:

Prior to starting your cannabis production endeavor, take the time to conduct extensive study and make thoughtful plans. The following framework will position you for success and assist you in avoiding frequent pitfalls:

Cultivar Selection: Spend some time learning about various cannabis cultivars and taking into account their growth characteristics, potency, and intended effects. Select cultivars that are compatible with your objectives, tastes, and the available cultivation conditions.

Growing Methods: Investigate a variety of growing methods, including hydroponic, indoor, and outdoor cultivation, among others. Think about the area, resources, and degree of participation you are comfortable with. Choose a method based on your needs because each one has pros and disadvantages.

Resources and Cultivation Guides: Make use of the abundance of knowledge found in forums, internet databases, and cultivation guides that are specifically devoted to cannabis. These tools offer insightful information, helpful hints, guidance for solving problems, and a helpful network of seasoned growers.

Patience and Perseverance:

It takes perseverance and patience to grow cannabis. To stay motivated and focused, bear in mind the following important points:

Learn from Mistakes: Recognize that making mistakes is a necessary component of learning. Accept them as opportunities for development and learning. Consider what went wrong, modify your strategy, and use the knowledge gained in later growth.

Understanding Growth Cycles: Cannabis plants go through various growth stages and need time to mature, so cultivating the plant requires patience. Don't rush the procedure; let the plants grow as they will. Every level provides many opportunities for learning.

Adaptability: Be ready to modify your plans as necessary to meet the unique requirements of your plants. Keep an eye out for changes in the environment, nutrient needs, and pest management, and act accordingly. Being adaptive is essential for success in cultivation because it is a dynamic process.

Learning from Experience:

Your cultivation journey will offer priceless teaching opportunities. Accept them and work to continually enhance your abilities:

Keep Thorough Records: Keep a cultivation journal to note important details such cultivar choice, planting dates, growth benchmarks, feeding regimens, pest control strategies, and yield data. This knowledge develops into a useful resource for future development.

Analyze and Reflect: Consistently analyze your cultivation experiences to pinpoint areas for development and possible technique improvements. The key to improving your cultivation techniques is to continuously learn from both successful and bad grows.

Experimentation: As you develop expertise, feel free to try out various cultivation strategies, feeds, training regimens, or lighting arrangements. You can learn what works best for your individual circumstances and cultivar choice with this hands-on approach.

Look for Resources and Support:

Don't be afraid to ask for help and make use of the resources at your disposal to improve your cultivation journey:

Community Involvement: Interact with other growers in person or online communities. Participate in forums, go to courses or events devoted to growing, and ask seasoned growers for guidance. The cannabis production community grows and develops a sense of brotherhood by exchanging information and experiences.

Professional Consultation: If necessary, think about speaking with knowledgeable experts, including horticulturists or cannabis consultants, who may offer specialized advice and support catered to your cultivation objectives and difficulties.

Local Regulations and Compliance: Be aware of any local rules or guidelines that apply to the production of cannabis. To make sure you are aware of and follow the appropriate regulations, get in touch with local authorities, business associations, or legal professionals.

Embracing the Joy of Cultivation:

Finally, never forget to enjoy growing your own cannabis plants:

Enjoy the Process: Growing marijuana may be a highly satisfying and fun activity. Enjoy the satisfaction of taking care of plants, seeing them flourish, and reaping the rewards of your labor. Honor the distinctive scents, tastes, and impacts that each cultivar offers.

Develop Mindfulness: Engaging in cultivation offers the chance to connect with nature and develop mindfulness. Spend time observing and caring for your plants while immersing yourself in gardening's therapeutic benefits.

Share Your Success: Tell others about your cultivation journey and your experiences. Celebrate your accomplishments, motivate other producers, and aid in the cannabis cultivation industry's expansion.

In conclusion, it takes meticulous planning, effort, patience, and a willingness to learn from experience for a novice grower to begin the adventure of cannabis production. You may face the difficulties and grow cannabis with assurance and joy by adopting the advice and inspiration offered in this section. Keep in mind that growing plants from seed to harvest is a lifelong learning process, ask for help from the growing community, and savor the benefits. May your efforts to produce cannabis provide you education, growth, and the satisfaction of producing your own crop.

Thank you for buying and reading/listening to our book.
If you found this book useful/helpful please take a few minutes
and leave a review on Amazon.com or Audible.com
(if you bought the audio version).

www.ingramcontent.com/pod-product-compliance
Lightning Source LLC
Chambersburg PA
CBHW050217070525
26309CB00012B/745